EVERYBODY WORKS IN SALES:

Here's what you need to know to achieve success in your career

by

Niraj Kapur

www.nirajkapur.com

Twitter: @Nirajwriter

This book is dedicated to those who work hard every day and don't get the recognition they deserve.

Contents

Introduction

We all work in sales. If you work for somebody, you earn a living by selling their product or service.

If you are self-employed, you earn a living by selling your product or service.

When you buy from Amazon, they always recommended other products similar to the ones you are purchasing or have already purchased - that's selling.

When you download a song, movie or TV show from iTunes, they always recommend more similar products. That's selling.

When you register for most websites, they sell their products or services to you through a regular email.

When you attend an exhibition at the NEC, London ExCel, Olympia, Manchester or even a local market, everyone is trying to sell you their product.

Other examples of selling include:

- When you're having a job interview.
- A child begging their parents for a present.
- Persuading your friends which restaurant or bar to go to.
- An advertising agency pitching for a client's business.
- A fitness trainer at the gym recommending how you work out.
- An internet entrepreneur promoting their course.
- A writer trying to find their next project.
- A musician searching for that next gig.
- A parent setting up a business to work around the school run.
- A manager asking his staff to work on a project.
- An employee asking their boss for a pay rise.
- A broadband company trying to sell their packages.
- A politician persuading you to vote.

Everyone is selling. A beautician doesn't just make you feel good, she sells beauty products and follow-up treatments. If you're a parent, you have to sell to your kids, especially teenagers who are surprisingly similar to difficult clients. When you buy a flight, the airline tries to sell you insurance, car rental and accommodation. Even on trains, they try to sell you refreshments and WIFI upgrades.

Most of us don't realise we're sales people, since sales people don't have the best reputation. When people think of sales, they think of one or all of the following:

1. Leonardo DiCaprio in the movie The Wolf of Wall Street - lying, taking drugs, uttering profanities, and leading a life of sexual debauchery.

2. Alex Baldwin in the movie Glengarry Glen Ross with his ruthless "Always Be Closing Manifesto" and bellowing "Coffee is for Closers." A real dinosaur from the 1980s and 1990s, uttered by managers who don't know what they're doing.

3. Gil, the nerdy loser from The Simpsons, who is always desperate for a sale.

4. Del Boy from Only Fools and Horses, a lovable rogue who will say and do anything to make a sale.

5. The door-to-door salesperson who disrupts your private time at home to sell you something you don't need.

6. The even more annoying person who calls your mobile and informs you that you've been in a car crash in the last five years (which you haven't) and would like to offer their services.

7. The sleazy car salesman who will do anything to get a commission.

Most professions require a degree or apprenticeship ensuring hard work for a number of years, yet anyone can apply for a sales job and all they get on average is 1-2 days of training. 1-2 days!

How much can you really learn in such a small amount of time?

1-2 days can never compare to the regular learning and studying that an apprenticeship or degree provides. Companies that offer week-long training are better, but still not enough.

That's why sales people have such a bad reputation, most of them are not properly trained.

The best sales people I have met read books on their speciality, invested in training courses, learned from their mistakes, learned on the job, wanted to help others and were a pleasure to deal with.

I've worked in sales in London since 1994. Having started off at the bottom and struggled for many years, I've achieved success, won multiple awards, made mistakes, been made redundant, been fired while on holiday, struggled with unemployment and risen from the ashes to achieve more success than I could ever have imagined.

If I can do it, anyone can with the right knowledge behind them and daily habits imbued in them. That's how this book can help you.

I have no superpowers. I'm not a child of privilege. I never went to a private school or a top university. I never even made it to university, yet everyone I have ever managed or out-earned had a degree.

Many account managers, strategic directors, commercial directors, estate agents, pharmaceutical reps, wholesalers, market traders, teachers, politicians, receptionists, business owners, all work in sales, yet so few know how to sell.

Sales is not just about commission on top of your salary. It's about serving the customer, engaging, learning, growing, dealing with tough times, facing colossal pressure, stressful days and you often have to attend a networking event, sometimes 2-3 nights in a row.

I will be sharing the insight and lessons I've learned so you can sell better, make your customers happier and earn a better living.

After all, who wants to:

- Earn more money?
- Be better at their job?
- Have more independence?

- Enjoy a letter lifestyle?
- Do better as an entrepreneur?
- Have a career?
- Gain more recognition from colleagues and respect from the boss?

This book is designed to help you.

Chapter One

Imagine working in an office with no individual computers or laptops, no internet, no email, no mobile phones, a CRM system where everything is on badly handwritten A5 cards, you have to ask a secretary to type up a proposal to fax to a client and there's no air conditioning in the summer. Welcome to 1994.

On the plus side, few people invested in exhibitions or conferences, since magazines were the most popular way for businesses to advertise. How times would change and obliterate so many businesses.

Companies used to advertise jobs in The Evening Standard newspaper as follows:

"Our top sales person earned £2,000 last week."

Do you know how amazing life would be with that kind of money?

I was born in Belfast and my family are Indian. As a struggling, out of work actor who couldn't find any roles for Indians or people with Irish accents, the future was bleak. The TV and movie industry was more stuck up and less accepting of ethnic actors in the 1990s. Today we have Indians on Netflix, being the love interest in Doctor Foster, in HBO Shows and yes, even the amazing Star Wars: Rogue One.

I struggled to fit into working-class Northern Ireland and spent all my time daydreaming, watching movies and listening to fun-loving long-haired 80s rock.

So, £2,000 a week sounded appealing. I left my small town in Northern Ireland to seek my fortune. A small town where everybody knew my name and I wished they didn't. A small town where most people hadn't travelled much outside their little bubble. I was going to show all the girls who turned me down at school and all the bullies who tormented me because of the colour of my skin that was I was going to make it in the big city.

After a ten-minute interview, Sterling Publications in Edgware Road, London offered me a job. It was my first interview. Looking back, if someone offers you a job after ten minutes, avoid them like the plague. I was given an A4 script, told to learn it and I was on the phone within the hour.

100 young people, mainly men, were crammed into a room with dreams of being a millionaire.

On the first day, several left, by end of the week, another twenty failed to return. When a customer would ask a question or give an objection, I was not trained on the product, so I kept reading the script.

To make matters worse, I was selling a gun magazine with a strong Belfast accent. Back when the IRA was terrorising the country, the last thing any self-respecting English person wanted to do was be sold advertising from someone with an accent like mine.

A few English people even begged me not to harm them!

They would often apologise and eventually hang up. I left my first real job after eight days.

That's how tough sales is. Rejection all day.

The next sales job advertised in The Evening Standard.

"Our top sales person earned £1,000 in a week!"

Another disaster. Reciting a script with 40 mins of training. Yes, 40 mins!

We didn't give the customer a chance to speak and were rejected within 60 seconds, usually 30 seconds. All day, every day. What a humiliation.

I didn't know anybody in sales and none of my family were in sales – they were normal people with normal jobs. With nobody to advise me and no internet to get advice from, I only lasted a few days at that nameless faceless company.

Luckily, Centaur, a well-known publishing house, advertised a job where they offered proper sales training. The salary was only £10,000 a year, (approx. $15,000 a year).

The week-long course was fun, learning about questions to ask clients (what makes you better than your competitor?) and closing techniques (would you like to run your advertisement for 6 weeks or 12 weeks?) and actually helping the client (how else can I support your business?)

My manager at the time, Brendan something-or-other, never did call coaching, never had a meeting with me and never questioned what I learned in my week's training. So, a few weeks later, I forgot all I learned.

LESSON 1. LEARN YOUR CRAFT AND KEEP ON LEARNING EVERY DAY.

The Business Manager, a bearded bear of a man who once told my friend to "fuck off and die" because he interrupted him at work, was a fountain of sales knowledge – he simply didn't know how to express it in the best way. Since I couldn't sell, he told me I was going to be fired. So, I played the pity card.

I left my small town in Northern Ireland to come to the big scary city of London. I have no friends or family, which is leading to serious depression – getting fired would destroy me.

The Business Manager's wife was an actress, so he understood the struggle of finding work and decided to give me a chance with a few days of sales training. His deep booming voice was like Darth Vadar standing over me, although Darth Vadar was friendlier.

The Business Manager taught me all the basics in those days.

- AIDA (Attention, Interest, Desire, Action).
- SPIN (Situation, Problem, Implication, Need pay-off).
- Persistence. Make more calls than anybody else.

Picking up the phone and calling customers for the first time is terrifying. Your voice trembles. Your throat goes dry. Your heart beats at a loud thump and you wish it was over. Pretty much like having your first date.

Like anything, practice makes perfect. When you have to pay rent and food and lots of bills, it's amazing how much effort you make.

Within a few weeks, picking up the phone became natural. I still spoke

13

too fast, however, it was indoors and I was working in central London which is an amazing place to be. I was earning commission and being a classified sales executive didn't seem so bad. I ended up with £4,000 commission on top of my tiny £10,000 basic salary.

That kind of money gets you nothing nowadays, but when you're single in the 1990s, it just about got me by. More important, it gave me the confidence to do better, and that's the inspiration you need to do better things.

So many people are scared of trying new things, but unless you try, you never know how far you can get.

In the 1990s, many people had 2-3 hour boozy lunches with clients, long smoking breaks and nobody ever took work home...

... so, I worked harder than anyone, took work home, never had more than 30 mins for lunch and spent 15 mins a day reading and re-reading my sales notes.

There was no distraction from mobile, internet or social media, so you wouldn't believe how much work I got done - within 3 years, my salary had increased by 100% and my commission by 200%.

My life was starting to make sense.

RECAP

- Learn every day. It will improve your life.
- Get proper training. If a company doesn't offer you ongoing training, they're wasting your time and you should look elsewhere.
- If you can't leave your job due to your financial circumstances, I understand. Many of us dislike our jobs, yet stay in them to pay the bills – so take matters into your own hands and invest in yourself. That's what successful people do.

"I do not think much of a man who is not wiser today than he was yesterday." – **Abraham Lincoln**

"Learning is the beginning of wealth. Learning is the beginning of health. Searching and learning is where the miracle process all begins." **– Jim Rohn, author of The Keys to Success and The Art of Exceptional Living**

Chapter Two

Being single can be a real struggle. If you're attractive, it's fun. If you're rich, it's fun. If you're rich and attractive, I can't stand you. But seriously, it's tough if you haven't grown up in London and don't have looks or money.

I had love handles you could hang a washing line on, acne in all the wrong places, national health glasses and was dressed by my father, so the odds weren't good.

Earning money was nice on payday, however, when you have nobody to spend it with, what's the point? I wasn't smart enough in my twenties to care about others the way I do now; if only I knew back then that giving to others was the secret to happiness.

To make matters more complicated, dating agencies were also taboo.

Now everybody single uses dating agencies. Back in the 1990s, I was mocked for being desperate and pathetic. Being stood up on a Friday or Saturday night in a restaurant is a truly humiliating experience, there were no mobiles to be rejected on by text. You sat there, all alone, waiting... while couples were having a great time.

I'll always be grateful to the staff at Bella Italia Leicester Square who eventually recognised me and would bring me free bread and a drink when I was stood up.

Finally, my parents told me to stop messing about and meet a nice Indian girl – I had nothing to lose, so why not? I would visit a different Indian family every weekend and you'd think I'd meet the right woman? Wrong.

I met her overprotective clichéd father and/or brother. These are the kind of stupid and intrusive questions they asked:

- How much money do you earn?
- Do you own a house?
- How many kids are you going to have?

- What car do you drive?
- What savings do you have?
- Have you ever been with a white woman before?
- How much money will you earn in the future?

The similarity to sales is incredible. Ask lame questions, get nowhere. Ask important questions, you will do well for yourself.

Here are the important questions they NEVER asked.

a) Will you treat my sister/my daughter with respect?

b) Will you always show love and kindness?

c) Will you be there through the good and bad times?

d) What kind of moral values do you have?

e) How do you treat the current members of your family?

I've bumped into many Indian women who rejected me at various weddings and functions over the years. They're either unhappily married to a jerk in a nice car or they're miserable, single and still living at home with their parents.

There's a lot to be said about that.

It's also a timely reminder for the future. What worked for decades does not work in the future as well. Goodbye Kodak, Blockbuster, Sony Ericsson and Woolworths.

After deciding that arranged marriage wasn't for me, I met Pia, a tall Scandinavian make-up artist. Nobody could understand why a tall, beautiful, mysterious blonde woman from Norway would be interested in me. Neither did I, but I wasn't going to complain. Maybe she thought I was somebody else. Again, I wasn't going to complain. It was a whirlwind romance and the first place I took her was Bella Italia in Leicester Square.

Congratulatory pats on the back followed from the waiters and waitresses. After being stood up and spending so many nights alone, happiness was finally coming my way.

I helped her find work on a short movie a friend of mine, TAM was

17

directing – yes, that was his nickname, Trouble At Mill. It should have warned me something bad was about to happen, but when you're in love, you often don't see the warning signs.

Pia was working on set and was too tired to see me during the short movie. So, I decided to surprise her one day with flowers and chocolates over lunch. When I strutted on the movie set of the Edgar Allen Poe project, you could hear a pin drop.

Everyone avoided eye contact. My strut became a walk, then a slouch. Something was wrong.

An elderly woman approached and asked me to leave. I couldn't understand why. She said that Pia was no longer interested in me and was having an affair behind my back. I was devastated.

I asked to speak with them, but she said to allow Pia and her son, TAM, some privacy. I lost my energy and strength. It was so humiliating,

Self-pity, eating myself into a sugar coma and swearing I would never fall in love again followed fast and hard. I lost track of time and the next thing I knew it was November and Christmas was around the corner. The thought of spending yet another Christmas alone was unbearable.

So, I decided to escape London and go somewhere I never thought I would go. A place that changed my life. I spent Christmas 1997 in India and ended up marrying a woman I knew for 20 minutes.

We all make mistakes when we're lonely. When desperation becomes so unbearable you end up talking to yourself on Saturday night for company. Or even worse, visiting the Samaritans which I did for many years on Marshall Street, Soho, just to have someone who would listen and stop me from killing myself. They're an amazing charity and I'm so grateful they were there to listen.

So, when I was 25 years old, I met 18-year-old Shweta in India.

We sat in a small room, both nervous, in her industrial smoggy town of Ghaziabad, one hour drive from New Delhi, where everyone beeps their horn when driving. She had large brown eyes, long dark hair and was stunning. Pia had broken my heart, so I wasn't going to focus on looks, I wanted kindness and authenticity.

I was relieved Shweta wanted to have kids. She had no money so didn't ask me stupid questions about my salary and how big my house was. Similarly, I would get no dowry which is common in Indian marriages where the woman's family gives a "financial gift" varying from a new bedroom, to a lump sum of money, to a car.

Shweta also spoke good English and was an amazing cook. She liked The Simpsons, enjoyed movies and wanted to get married and have kids.

So, after 20 minutes, I agreed to marry her.

LESSON 2 - PERSISTENCE LEADS TO LUCK WHICH LEADS TO SUCCESS.

Four days later on our wedding day, 600 people I had never met in my life turned up. 600 people I didn't know! It was so scary.

All those years of getting my heart broken and being humiliated, as a teen, then as an adult... but I never gave up. I believed in love and was convinced it would make me happy.

When you want something, go after it with your heart and soul. You endure the pain, learn from mistakes, believe in the impossible and persist.

After years of heartbreak, loneliness and rejection, I had got what I wanted. Yes, I did it in the most unusual way - unusual by western society's standards - but a win is a win.

RECAP

- It's an oldie, but a goodie: Never give up.
- Good opportunities come your way if you have faith and persist. Nothing happens when you whine and complain about it.

"Perseverance is failing 19 times and succeeding the 20th." – **Julie Andrews**

"To the doubters and naysayers and everyone who gave me hell and said I could not, that I would not or I must not – your resistance made me stronger, made me push harder, made me the fighter that I am today. It made me the woman that I am today. So, thank you." – **Madonna**

Chapter Three

Marriage created more success in my life. I had security and came home every night to fresh, delicious mouth-watering Indian food from Shweta. Not that chicken tikka and poppadum nonsense you get in most curry houses, I'm talking authentic, moreish flavours that aren't dripping in oil.

At the beginning, it was tough. Shweta left everything behind and flew thousands of miles from New Delhi to London. Unfortunately, India was not full of billionaires and millionaires like it is now. Not many people had travelled, so their experience of the world was through Bollywood movies. Here's what they all thought:

- Everyone in London lived in a mansion.
- English people spoke like the Queen.
- Everyone was singing and dancing.

In the rough working-class, South Harrow council estate which was the only place I could afford a mortgage, here was the reality:

- If you attempted conversation, people thought you were weird and avoided you.
- If you smiled, people would look at you with utter confusion.
- Everyone sounded like Ray Winstone.
- Single mums on benefits wore nicer clothes that my wife.
- Children on benefits wore nicer clothes than I did.

Singing and dancing was the staple of all Indian movies in the 1990s and a way of bringing people together. Nobody in London sang apart from when the football World Cup or Euros were in full swing and everyone would join in: "Engerlaaaannndd."

Living with someone you don't know is scary, especially when you realise you have little in common.

Shweta and I had never lived with anyone before. We had no family nearby supporting us and I found it hard making friends in London. I

21

knew so many people, had hundreds of acquaintances, but no friends.

We realised it wasn't going to work. I was too scared to tell my father who would beat the crap out of me. Shweta was too scared to tell her mother who would have brought massive shame on her community to have a divorced daughter... we joked about it and decided we would do everything we could to make it work.

I wanted to give my wife the best of everything, not a rundown terraced house and second-hand car.

I quit my first proper job at Centaur and went to work long hours in the city for a financial company.

Mark the boss was friendly, professional, seemed like the perfect employer. Then on day two, he told me he was going travelling and had resigned. I was gutted. Having a good boss makes such a big difference in your career.

His replacement was Paul, a tall northerner who was unable to connect with me because I didn't listen to Oasis or support Man Utd, but as he was the most experienced after Mark, he got the job.

It's scary how many people become managers like this.

Go for the best person? No, most companies avoid paying a recruitment consultancy to find somebody excellent and instead, hire someone internally with no people skills or management experience. After all, it saves money and sadly, that's what most companies care about.

Although Paul lasted several years and has done well for himself since, he wasn't a great boss. He never encouraged, only criticised. There's an old saying: "people don't leave companies, they leave bad managers."

When I complained about Paul's behaviour, I expected support from the powers that be. They did nothing. Not a damn thing.

I've seen this happen to so many people. I've heard about this happening to hundreds of people. Another appalling thing companies do, they defend managers when they should not be defended.

I had just become a father and it didn't help that once or twice a week

I would fall asleep at my desk. You get up once a night with a crying baby, you don't fall asleep straight away and you're shattered the next day. That's why I always sympathise with new parents, it's exhausting.

When managers make you feel inferior, it's hard, almost impossible to focus on the job. All I could think about was the rich clients I had and the hundreds of millions of pounds profit they made. If I had that money, I wouldn't need to deal with a terrible boss. Being rich seems like a perfect world. This is what I thought about rich people at the time.

a)   They lead better lives.

b)   They are always happy.

c)   They never have to worry.

d)   They have no morals and prey on the weak, but I would be different.

I started playing the lottery, spending £10, then £20, then £100 a week convinced I would win, but all that happened was I got into serious debt.

LESSON 3 – DON'T LET MONEY RUIN YOUR LIFE.

I came to my senses... then had another money-making idea.

Watching the popular TV Show, Who Wants To Be A Millionaire? I found myself shouting the answers at the TV.

The contestant failed. I could have £32,000 in my pocket if I was on that show.

My obsession with money continued, thinking of all the nice holidays, designer clothes and expensive restaurants I could eat at. So during breakfast, lunch and on the daily commute to work, I studied every quiz book, convinced I would win big.

It started off well, £600 on ITV's The Biggest Game Show in Town. £3,000 on Sky One show, Dirty Money. That paid for a lot of nappies and baby food. Then I got cocky and appeared on The Weakest Link.

The previous two shows were wonderful, had a great crew and lovely contestants. The Weakest Link was awful.

1. Contestants tried to stitch one another up.
2. An entire day on set, then filming in the evening, making it a 14-hour day.
3. You got paid nothing.
4. The BBC wouldn't even pay my full travel expenses.

There's also rule on primetime TV – never say "pass."

My legs wobbled, the tension got the worst of me and I forgot answers to lots of simple questions. Finally, when Anne Robinson asked me what the NUJ stood for, it was simply "National Union of Journalists." I couldn't think of the answer and couldn't pass, so I blurted out "National Union of Jugglers."

The audience laughed. Anne Robinson didn't. She gave me one of her hard stares.

At the end of the round, I expected witty banter that made the show famous. Instead, Anne sat down with someone, maybe a comedy writer and came back five mins later with banter.

Not what I was expecting. She gave me a deservedly hard time and I then had to do the walk of shame from three different angles.

I was The Weakest Link.

My obsession with money had ruined a year of my life.

When you're broke, you're convinced money is the key to happiness. Money is so addictive, but like my father always said, "unless you inherit money, you have to work your guts out to earn it. There's no easy way. If there was, someone would have told us by now."

I went back to my job at the financial company the next day and realised that I had made a mistake by focusing on how to earn money. Paul didn't care.

He bonded with his team and left me out. Was it racism? Hard to say. I don't like to blame the colour of my skin for my failures, so I will give him the benefit of the doubt and say that wasn't it.

Sometimes people just don't get on with each other.

Staff at the financial company were friendly and they stood for taking financial matters into your own hands. They were a good company, I just wasn't the right hire. Until I put pen to paper, I don't think I have ever admitted that before.

I was making £20,000 a month on sales for them, so shortly after I left through their lack of support, there were redundancies.

At the same time, thousands of people were losing their jobs as the internet bubble burst and people found out that owning millions of pounds of stock in internet companies meant nothing.

Although the internet proved to be an excellent investment long-term, getting sucked into the next big thing and the chance to earn millions, was a poor choice.

With no job, I called recruitment companies asking for work. I took every job interview that came my way. Trying to find a job is hard work. Trying to find a job when you're unemployed is such a miserable experience. After two months of getting nowhere or being offered roles that were not my cup of tea, I went back begging to Centaur and they kindly gave me back my old job.

RECAP

- Don't let money ruin your life.
- Money is addictive, so be careful with your choices.
- Never rush into anything.

"If you want to know what God thinks of money, just look at the people he gave it to." – **Dorothy Parker, writer, poet, critic, satirist**

"My formula for success is to rise early, work late and strike oil." – **JP Getty**

Chapter Four

I was welcomed back to Centaur with open arms. In addition to selling advertising in magazines, Annie, the publisher, gave me the chance to sell existing yearbooks and launch new yearbooks. The task was monumental; do my 9-5 job selling advertising and sell advertising into yearbooks on top.

The stakes were high. Up to £2,200 bonus per month. I wanted to give my daughter what she needed. My relationship with my father was intense growing up and I didn't plan to be in the office working all the time... however, when you want something, I didn't know how to achieve it without back-breaking hard work.

Working Saturdays with Shweta sending faxes – companies rarely get faxes over the weekend, so I figured contacting people on Saturday would show my resilience and it worked. I would type up sales mailers, simple, short, to the point, highlighting the benefits of working with us.

Too many sales people, and far too many marketers, sell features. Nobody cares. Selling is about how the customer benefits, not what features you offer.

Launching anything new is a hard task. Take a look at the stats I've uncovered after years of new business launches.

- Let's say you make 40 calls a day.
- 20 people are in meetings or out of the office – frustrating.
- 10 people are in the office, they just don't want to speak with you – equally frustrating.
- 8 people reject your project – unbelievably frustrating.
- 2 clients are interested – you adore these clients and consider including them in your will.

Depressing stats, so you need to be surrounded by positive people.

It was 3-4 late nights, plus every Saturday.

However, it was exhausting, with Shweta supporting me on Saturdays, it made a huge difference. It was fun bonding with her, so I decided to enlist the help of my colleagues in the office during the week since Shweta wasn't there.

I couldn't pay them commission, however, when I got commission at the end of the month, I bought them pastries and took them out for lunch at the end of each project to say thank you.

Sabeena Atchia always told great jokes and made sure everything ran on time.

Geoff Ball, the softly spoken production manager and my first gay friend, chased up all the artwork.

Gordon Palmer had an insane laugh and brought so much positive energy to the office to match the young talented kids on the block, Simon Yandell and Bill Maclachlan.

The remarkable Debbie Rimmer made sure everything ran smoothly. My boss, John Scarrott, who would spend all day quoting David Brent from the TV show The Office, was pushing me to do my best and smash the revenue targets.

Even the publisher Annie, chipped in and got associations to buy pages and recommended the yearbooks to their members at a discount.

Suba in the post room would carry extra postbags of my mailers and high-five me every day.

In the exhibitions team, Melissa Wattam, a crazy, brilliant American, who was competing with me as best sales person, was working with John "JK" Kinoshi who looked like a gangster and was one of the nicest guys you could ever meet. (Melissa eventually beat me to sales person of the year). Both offered incredible support every day along with the wonderful, kind Marva Hudson who always told me I could do it.

Working as a team creates more energy, more enthusiasm, it gives you hope on a Friday afternoon at 4.00pm, when all you want to do is stop working and hit the pub.

<u>LESSON 4 - SURROUNDED YOURSELF WITH GREAT PEOPLE.</u>

There's no way I could do this by myself. Working with amazing people who support you and care about you makes all the difference.

As important as these wonderful people are, be careful of the ones who distract you.

If someone gossips, avoid them.

If someone criticises colleagues behind their back, avoid them.

If someone complains about yet another charity bake sale to raise money for a good cause, avoid them.

If someone complains about the news and state of the world, smile politely and avoid them.

Every office has these people. They will suck away your energy and time, two vital factors you need, not just for success, but for everyday living.

The only exceptions are if someone complains about their boss since there are so many bad bosses around and if someone complains about their health or the health of a loved one – that requires a lot of care and understanding,

Jim Rohn, considered by many to be the founder of personal development, and one of my heroes once said "you become the average of the five people you spend time with."

Looking back on my life I can say this is 100% true. When I hung out with losers, I was a loser. When I spent time with people who were kind and supportive, I became kind and supportive to others.

Positivity sounds very American and not that British, however, it's a vital component of everyday success.

Just shy of turning 30, I enjoyed my work and was making a decent living, because I surrounded myself with positive people. Those who struggled blamed the government and the banks for all their problems and were stuck in the same jobs with the same salaries for years.

RECAP

- You can always go further in a group than by yourself.
- Surround yourself with positive people.

- Even Steve Jobs, Mark Zuckerberg and Bill Gates, the most successful people in the world, had groups of people advise and support them.

"Surround yourself with those who only lift you higher." – **Oprah Winfrey**

"Everyone is your best friend when you are successful. Make sure that the people that you surround yourself with are also the people that you are not afraid of failing with." – **Paula Abdul**

Chapter Five

Becoming a parent is the greatest thing that will ever happen to you. Sort of.

One to two-year-olds; you look like a zombie from lack of sleep. Kids pick up every illness. It's important for their immune system, however, you also pick up lots of the illnesses, don't sleep and look hungover.

Three to ten-year-olds; It's pure magic. Happiest years of my life. Daughters have a special bond with their fathers and I feel so blessed that our daughter was healthy and happy and made everyone's life better.

11-year-olds; they start raising their voices and pointing fingers. You think it will pass. 12-year-olds; it doesn't pass and they then start to tut, moan, complain and whine. 13-year-olds; you want to give them up for adoption.

You sacrifice everything for your kids and they don't appreciate anything you do. They talk back, ignore you in public and never listen to a word you say. Having your child ignore you in public and walk in the opposite direction takes years of therapy and ice-cream to get over.

Apparently, they come around about 17-years-old. Much of this relates to the workplace and working in sales.

From the age of three, being a father is amazing. With mothers, it's amazing from day one, because you've carried the baby inside you and maybe breastfed as well, that creates a special bond – plus most women I know are naturally more caring than men, who often cancel attending their kid's parent's evening if their favourite football team are playing.

The joy of holding your kid's hand, teaching them to read, play sport, watch movies, bowl, ice-skate, shop for clothes, these are moments to be cherished. Why? Because you're showing unconditional love to someone.

I tried that with my clients. Not the hand-holding and kisses on the cheek before bed, but the caring and wanting to make a difference. And what a difference it made.

Clients now saw me as a value creator. Instead of calling and pitching, I would send an article and recommended they read it.

a)   I sent them thank you cards after a meeting.

b)   Birthday cards.

c)   Christmas cards.

99% of people don't send thank you or birthday cards, even Christmas cards are becoming a lost tradition, yet these simple techniques made me stand head and shoulders above the competition and often ensured the customer did business with me longer because I made them feel special. I genuinely cared.

I once recommend my client attend an event by a competitor to find new customers because I thought the competitor ran a decent show. Most people don't do this, but the client will love you for it. I introduced clients to other clients to help each other. I would travel 1-2 hours to see clients every month and take them out for a nice lunch, not to sell them, to say thank you for giving me your business, to see how I could help then, share new ideas and learn more about their business. Not once did I ask for anything in return.

Too many people take from customers. Equally worse, many people do something nice for a customer, then immediately demand something in return.

LESSON 5 – CARE FOR PEOPLE AND ASK FOR NOTHING IMMEDIATELY IN RETURN.

This extends to helping colleagues in the office, helping a friend and giving to charity.

Karma is a beautiful thing. If you give care and expect nothing, love and goodwill will always come back to you.

The comic genius and Oscar-winning actor Robin Williams often visited hospitals unannounced; no press, no publicity, just to make the patients feel special. Robin was a wonderful human being who made an enormous impact on the world, not just because he was a world-class entertainer, but because of how he cared for others and the hundreds of millions of dollars he raised for Comic Relief USA with Whoopi Goldberg and Billy Crystal.

<u>RECAP</u>

- Being caring never goes out of style.
- Being unselfish will never go out of fashion.

"My guiding principles in life are to be honest, thoughtful, loving and caring." – **Prince William**

"Never be so busy as not to think of others." – **Mother Teresa**

Chapter Six

Albert Einstein once famously said *"insanity is doing the same thing over and over and over and expecting a different result."*

I stopped improving. I stopped challenging myself.

I had no idea that personal development or self-improvement was even a thing. For a few months, I just stopped caring.

To make matters worse, management expected too much from me and I was stuck in a rut. It happens to all of us.

Considering we spend more time in work than with friends, family or hobbies, shouldn't we enjoy work more?

Teddy Colmson, a former Centaur colleague, who was a renegade rock n roller who played by his own rules, asked me to join him in a new business venue in East London.

In 2018, Shoreditch is trendy, has cool bars, delicious restaurants, money and clubs. In 2004, it had none of these.

Teddy sold me the benefits of working in a non-corporate environment.

1) I could wear a t-shirt and jeans to work.

2) East London was going to be the coolest part of London in the future.

3) Together we could make history.

We've all met someone who could sell ice to the eskimos, well that was Teddy, so I agreed to be part of his sales organisation.

We started selling a charity fundraising event for the Down's Syndrome Association. Since my mother was a physio, I've met kids with Down's Syndrome, who are among the kindest people you could ever meet - supporting them was a privilege. We sold tables and advertising into a book-of-the-night. Honourable work, however, it didn't pay the bills.

With my wife running her business in Buckingham, I understand the struggles and challenges of small business owners, with high rent, overheads, tax and government red tape. My wife is considered by her clients to be not just the best in Buckinghamshire, but a world-class beauty therapist - although it took her several years to get there. We didn't have several years. We lived month by month.

Luckily, a former colleague, Dean Wattam (who was married to the fabulous American Melissa from Marketing Week) a macho, ginger Yorkshireman, was leaving his post at The Guardian to retire in Spain. Not bad for your mid-30s. He kindly recommended me to sell The Guardian Media Handbook, which was a who's who of the British media industry.

We got paid a retainer to cover my salary plus a percentage of the sales, but how much commission can you make just selling an advert in a thick handbook. It was 40-50 calls per day, 5 days a week and although we made profit for The Guardian, it wasn't enough.

Sometimes, you just need luck, and like I said in chapter two, persistence leads to luck which leads to success.

Jonathan Viner, a 6' 6" likeable business development manager was impressed by my work ethic and recommended me to Charlotte Gooch, an intelligent, ambitious head of events at The Guardian who hired us to sell an annual public sector conference that needed a sponsor. It was called the Oxford Media Convention and was routinely opened by the head of culture, media and sport from the British government, so it was a huge deal.

Companies travelled to the Said Business School in Oxford and paid over £500 to attend for a day.

This was big ticket with a £10,000 sponsorship tag, but we only had 4 weeks to sell it and we knew nothing about the public sector. It was impossible. But sometimes the impossible is sent to test us, and with no other income, what choice did we have?

We had no future work in the pipeline, so gave it a shot. Calling big companies to try and do business was a nightmare:

a)   They don't return voice mails.

b)   They don't return messages.

c)   They don't reply to emails.

Rather than calling every company in the public sector, I made a shortlist of 20 companies. KPMG was top of my list. I must have rung about 20 different people who were all going straight to voice mail but finally call number 20, I heard a familiar Northern Irish accent from the marketing manager. We talked about life back home and a meeting was promptly set up.

Two meetings and three weeks later, we had a sponsor. KPMG saved us with a £10,000 deal at the last minute.

The Guardian were delighted - a happy employer often leads to new opportunities - and they gave us a chance to sell a new event they were launching called The Guardian Media Summit, looking at the future of media such as downloading, mobile streaming and social media.

This was 2005 and something nobody had any knowledge of.

I called Microsoft, BT, BBC, ITV, YAHOO, AOL, all the big potential players in 2005. I don't even think Facebook or Google existed back then and nobody I knew was using Amazon.

The companies I approached knew technology was the future, they weren't too sure how. More importantly, The Guardian were talking about something everyone wanted more knowledge of.

No more £10,000 deals, these deals were £25,000 per partner and £50,000 for a headline sponsor.

So many valuable takeaways from pitching big companies:

LESSON 6 - WHEN YOU SPEAK, MAKE IT SUCCINCT AND PROVIDE VALUE.

- They get 50 - 100 calls per day from sales people trying to sell to them.

- Be able to get your value proposition across in 30 seconds or less. Don't tell them what you do. Customers don't care about you, they care about the value you provide.

- When you finally talk to a big company, they have heard everything, so respect their time and think of unique ways to communicate.

LESSON 7 - KEEP IT SIMPLE AND ALWAYS MAKE IT VISUAL.

- They rarely reply to sales emails because most of them are so badly written – full of features and no benefits, and are almost always far too long. Research shows people absorb visual images several times faster than having to read large chunks of writing.

LESSON 8 - LEARN TO WRITE SHORT, EFFICIENT EMAILS.

- Don't just speak to the marketing manager, speak to the marketing executive, communications manager, PR manager and commercial director, all these people are involved in the decision and quite often they have to sell it to the board.

LESSON 9 - HAVING MULTIPLE CONTACTS AT COMPANIES WILL ALWAYS HELP YOU MORE THAN JUST HAVING ONE CONTACT.

- You put the same effort getting £10,000 from someone as £50,000.

LESSON 10 - ALWAYS THINK BIG AND GO FOR THE BIGGER DEAL.

- I've had companies say no to me several times before I got a yes. Sometimes it's taken a few years to do a deal. No often means not right now. Research shows that 80% of people give up after two phone calls.

- 80% give up! Don't fall into that group.

- Research shows it takes 9-12 phone calls to reach a decision maker. That's what successful people do.

LESSON 11 - COMPANIES APPRECIATE PEOPLE WHO DON'T GIVE UP AND KEEP IN TOUCH, EVEN WHEN THEY'VE SAID NO.

Several incredibly tough and frustrating months later, we had secured almost £100,000 of sponsorship from BT and Microsoft.

Staff at The Guardian couldn't understand how we could sell so much.

Richard Branson gives lots of advice on how to succeed on LinkedIn. He never worries about people being more successful than him, since most people don't take good advice.

I advised so many Guardian sales people on the above lessons, yet they didn't listen, that's how much people hate change – so many would rather stay in their comfort zone and be average, than take risks, put in long hours and become successful.

You'd think people would be happy if you worked your socks off and achieved success at selling something that was unbelievably tough. Some people were, most weren't.

I never threw my success in their face and never bragged about it. I'm not a shouter and screamer, I prefer to lead by example. Yet some of the dirty looks I got. While success can breed success, it can also breed jealousy.

I can see why many people don't want success. Getting out of your comfort zone, working longer hours, sacrificing time with family, less time with friends, not having time to watch television, being disliked. Who wants that?

The difference between success and failure is several habits practised every day. That's it.

It's not where you were born or what school you went to. Some of the most successful people I have met went to local high schools and in some cases, avoided university completely. It's about great habits and implementing those great habits on a daily basis.

The Guardian Media Summit SOLD OUT. A massive success. Thirteen years later it's still the most popular and high profile event The Guardian runs. I'm very proud of that legacy.

Next year, we secured MTV and a variety of telecom and tech companies as sponsors, pushing past £130,000 in revenue.

Then we got offered more conference and event launches like the MEGA Innovation Awards.

So many sales people worked only in magazines. Or conferences. Or only awards.

Here I was selling exhibition stands, awards, conference sponsorship and digital.

Cross-selling across multiple platforms is becoming more common in 2017. It was way ahead of the curve in 2006 and becoming a multi-platform expert was the best thing I ever did. It was longer hours, bigger risks, scarier, however, the pay-off was magnificent.

The Guardian Public Sector Exhibition failed in 2010 due to a tube strike which meant people couldn't attend and the show flopped. Exhibitors were furious and not given proper customer care. There should have been replacement buses for visitors and taxis for VIP guests and speakers. So, I was asked to:

a)   Sell an event that had failed.

b)   Deal with angry customers over the phone.

c)   Deal with angry emails from customers.

d)   Generate £300,000 of revenue from exhibition stands and sponsorship.

e)   I did not want to do any of the above.

f)   I didn't even know how to do any of the above

Imagine you spend between £20,000 to £50,000 on an exhibition – that includes the stand design and build, travel, hotels for staff, brochures, food and drink and people didn't turn up. How would you feel? Who would you blame?

Whoever has the courage to pick up the phone and talk to you – which was me.

When I saw the mammoth task ahead, I hired Nick 'The Knife' Thomson to work with me. He was a hard grafter. We were like two gladiators out to fight a battle where we both had little chance of winning.

<u>RECAP</u>

- Be succinct and provide value.

- Keep presentations simple and make them visual.

- Write short emails with benefits to the customer.

- Have multiple contacts at every company.

- Think big.

"The sole purpose of business is service. The sole purpose of advertising is explaining the service which business renders." – **Leo Burnet, advertising innovator, founder Leo Burnett Agency**

"Corporate decision makers expect you to get yourself fully grounded about their business, industry, market trends, objectives, customers, competitors, and challenges." – **Jill Konrath, author More Sales Less Time and Agile Selling**

Chapter Seven

It's tough when customers condemn you for something that isn't your fault. They hate the company, but blame you. The previous sales people aren't there, they blame you. The organiser is too gutless to speak to them, they blame you.

People want to sell their products, however, I've learned that asking open questions and listening to what a client says is more important since that usually leads to the sale.

When people talk about business, they use words such as "relentless", "tenacity", "and "grit." One of the most underrated skills is listening.

What makes you successful at selling your product is deep listening. This is often through:

a) Tone.

b) Body language.

c) What isn't being said.

Tone and body language are easy to understand. Crossed arms and feet towards the door are never good signs. Anger tell you a lot. It takes a lot of experience to understand what isn't being said.

If someone isn't happy with their supplier, they might reply "they're okay" but how do they say it?

That's when you delve deeper and ask more questions. The client will respect you for caring and not selling which is what more people should try and do.

This slower sale builds respect among customers that have been disappointed in the past.

<u>LESSON 12 - LEARN TO LISTEN TO WHAT IS BEING SAID AND TO WHAT IS NOT SAID.</u>

I was never a master closer. I never forced the deal. I never had an answer for everything. I asked important questions that got people thinking, provided advice and listened.

At this stage, I'd been married 9 years. When you're married or in a relationship, you need to learn these skills as well, otherwise, you're in trouble.

One of the most dissatisfied customers I ever spoke to at The Guardian was Orange mobile (they've now merged with T-Mobile to become EE). Nobody ever listened to what they said. Sales people just tried to take money from them.

I met them for 1 hour. I spoke for less than 20 minutes and that was at the end. I asked questions about their business and listened deeply. I researched their business for hours beforehand to understood what they wanted.

That afternoon, I received a call thanking me for helping them and actually caring. A week later, they signed a £20,000 deal.

Every talented person I worked with at The Guardian was an excellent listener.

Gemma and Danielle Senior were tireless event managers who had to listen to problems all day. Charlotte Gooch cracked the whip hard. She was an excellent listener and now runs her own successful management consultancy.

Geoff Lippett oversaw the boring politics and paperwork that any good manager does. He was such a good listener, he would often pause thoughtfully when asked a question.

After several months of criticism from disgruntled exhibitors, long hours and listening like I was a professional therapist, we surpassed the £300,000 exhibition stand and sponsorship target to earn a whopping £375,000, plus an additional £100,000 of on-site rebookings.

Orange were a first-time sponsor, while top technology companies like LG were exhibiting. My first exhibition and we killed it.

Nick and I received our bonuses from Teddy and I bought a car (just to clarify, it was a Mazda 6 family car, not an expensive sports car) and returned to the office expecting a hero's welcome.

What happened next was a complete shock, something that was to destroy me in ways I never thought possible.

<u>RECAP</u>

- Listening is one of the best ways of doing business.
- People want to be heard.
- Listen to what is being said and more important, what isn't being said.

When people talk, listen completely. Most people never listen." – **Ernest Hemingway**

If speaking is silver, then listening is gold." – **Turkish proverb**

Chapter Eight

The Guardian was cutting jobs. According to the posters in the canteen, the CEO was given a massive bonus while so many people were made redundant, which created resentment among staff

The job cuts didn't surprise me. Every Monday, The Guardian produced a popular media supplement, which everyone read. It went from carrying 40 pages of advertising making over £100,000 per week to only 4 pages of advertising making only £10,000 per week.

Monster, Reed and various internet job sites were taking business from the newspapers. Guardian sales staff weren't prepared and many were not being trained enough to work in sales. I saw them take incoming calls and so many people didn't understand the art of learning your craft, cold calling or asking questions.

Nick Thomson and I were the top performers, so we would be safe. The director of Guardian Business and Professional was a huge supporter of ours for many years. He could always rely on us to deliver and was a fellow Northern Irishman, so I knew he would fight my corner.

Wrong.

He made a decision I've seen lots of senior executives make. They looked at how to save money short-term without thinking about long-term effects.

Nick and I were replaced by graduates who cost only £22,000 per year compared to my basic salary of £36,000.

For the sake of saving £28,000, The Guardian got rid of its two best performers. Loyal sales people who went to the ends of the earth, showed care and passion for the business, were replaced by two inexperienced sales people who were no good.

Because we had worked through the advertising sales house, as consultants, there was no pay off, no redundancy package and after five years of loyalty, The Guardian gave us nothing.

It's hard to describe the pain and anger when someone treats you like this. We were told The Guardian wanted to have staff in-house instead of outsourcing, however, when you are not appreciated for all the hard work and sacrifices you have made, it hurts.

What about the drinks sessions, lunches, team meetings, bonding over coffee, late nights working for the greater good? Surely after five years, someone would reach out, say thanks, maybe even give a job reference?

LESSON 13 - YOUR BOSSES ARE NOT YOUR FRIENDS.

Don't expect them to be there for you. It's often every person for themselves, especially when jobs are being cut.

Your bosses are not your friends. Your friends are your friends.

Managers, like most sales people, are badly trained. This is how most people become managers:

a) To save a company money from not hiring a recruitment consultancy.

b) Because it's easier.

c) They're mates with someone in a senior position.

These are terrible reasons to make someone a manager, yet they're how 70%-80% of managers are appointed. And most of them are not even trained!

As a result, the majority of managers work by instilling fear, (do this or else), or they are never around to face problems. Sound familiar?

Eventually I became a boss, (more on this later), and like being a writer, everyone thinks they can do it. The pressure is more intense, the stakes are greater and the higher up the chain you go, the more responsible you are.

Back to The Guardian...

There was no thank you cards, no farewell drinks, nobody even shook our hands.

They told us by email.

I expected so much more from The Guardian. The only comfort

we had was that in the following year, the young cheap sales people who replaced us were so awful the Guardian Public Sector Exhibition flopped and the event shut down. The Guardian lost hundreds of thousands of pounds, just so they could save £28,000 on salaries.

When terrible situations happen to us in life, it's important to remain calm, think things through, never make important decisions when you're emotional or desperate or both - and stop feeling sorry for yourself. Your mind will play games all day, mainly the negative kind.

Hindsight is a wonderful thing and I wish I could have done those things.

I was out of work and what followed next, well, I hope it never happens to anyone.

RECAP

- Don't ignore your friends or family, they will always be there. Your boss won't and your company never will.

- Your boss is there to get the best out of you. Most bosses don't know how to do this.

"People don't leave bad jobs, they leave bad bosses." – **Anon**

Chapter Nine

Hard times can make people do bad things:

a) Drink too much.

b) Live in denial

c) Take drugs.

d) Lose your temper.

e) Destroy friendships.

f) Hurt loved ones.

g) Blame your children for everything.

h) Steal.

i) Fight.

When things are going well, it's easy to be nice. When things are brutally hard, that's when someone's true colours follows.

Teddy went from being supportive and renegade to foul-mouthed, short-tempered and deeply unpleasant. Since he was his own boss, he hated being told what to do, especially when he was wrong. He turned up late for meetings and once placed his feet on the desk of a client to show "how cool" he was. It started to become genuinely embarrassing. The final straw was during a client meeting when he discussed politics.

When you have a client meeting, there are certain things you never do – discuss politics or sex, talk in a sexist, racist or homophobic manner or use profanity.

Here's what Teddy did. He uttered the word c**t to express his dislike for a member of the British government.

The client was speechless. And female. I was gobsmacked. Teddy grinned like he was a comic genius lighting up London's West End. The client relationship quickly deteriorated.

We weren't finding work and instead of supporting me, Teddy blamed me for everything. Looking back, I understand his frustration, however, if you want someone to perform better, putting them down and yelling makes no difference.

My confidence was at an all-time low after The Guardian made me redundant. I missed my colleagues and after five years, I was devastated than none of them kept in touch. Even worse, my good friend Nick did a deal behind our backs and went to work directly for The Guardian, you can imagine how we felt.

Teddy gave me three months notice and said that unless business came in, he would have to let me go. At the time, I thought it was cruel. Looking back, it was actually quite decent of him.

I've seen many employers throw people out when times get tough. Teddy kept me on for a few months while I went for interviews, so at least I could pay the bills. He didn't express himself in the best way and I never spoke to him again, although deep inside I think he did care.

I was the opposite, I expressed myself too much. Irish people are expressive and say what's on their mind. Indian people are expressive and say what's on their mind. What did you expect from me?

So I was 38-years-old and unemployed. Not a good statistic. Every interview I had, the following happened:

1. The person interviewing me was younger than me.

2. The person interviewing me was slimmer.

3. The person interviewing me had more hair.

In all fairness, most people I meet are slimmer and have more hair than me.

When you can't pay the bills, it gets worse. Desperation sets in and you make stupid decisions. My weight increased. Confidence faded. The glass was always half empty.

Walking around with a chip on my shoulder, I was pissed off at how I had been treated and frustrated with having no money.

Taking that into consideration, my reaction to being made unemployed was understandable, however, potential employers don't see it that way. They want someone they can work with, not some angry has-been.

The longer I was unemployed, the less money I had left and the angrier I felt. Money was running out...

Paying bills and supporting a family isn't easy when there's only one income. My wife's father passed away from cancer when she was young, so she was the main breadwinner in her family. In addition to running her own business, she was generously helping her brothers with university fees by working 7 days a week. We never saw each other until we went to bed exhausted and then we would fight since we were both tired and frustrated.

I blamed everyone for my problems. The government for making life too expensive. My parents for not bringing me up as well as they should have. My father for having no hair and enormous love handles. My wife for caring more about her brothers than paying our bills and worse of all, I blamed my daughter, just because she was the only one who would listen to me. My male ego was shattered and I was humiliated because I couldn't support my family.

LESSON 14 - IT'S NOT WHAT HAPPENS, IT'S HOW YOU REACT

The final straw was one day in traffic, someone accidentally drove into the wrong lane and I swerved, almost crashing my car. I was so frustrated that I sped ahead and rolled down my window and threatened to kill him with an avalanche of profanity. His kids were in the back of the car terrified.

The sound of frightened children made me realise what an idiot I had become.

I look back on this period of my life with enormous embarrassment. Three months of failure and look at what I had become. I simply couldn't cope.

My father flew over and spent a few days with us. He told me I was suffering from depression. My wife had been telling me this for months, but I never listened. At her beauty salon in Buckingham, most of her clients are successful women over 40, so they've had husbands go through mid-life crises. Some of them are still married, many are divorced and as a therapist, you spend all day long listening to people's problems.

I realised I needed to change, but didn't know how. Quite often in life when we need something, we get a signal. Call it what you like, a sign from God. Fate. Luck. Karma.

Then one day in WH Smith newsagents, I got the signal that changed my life.

RECAP

- Be careful how you react to awful situations.
- When something bad happens, take a moment, never react straight away.
- Decisions based in anger rarely lead to anything intelligent or productive.

"Life is 10% of what happens to me and 90% how I react to it." – **John Maxwell, leader, pastor, author of The 5 Levels of Leadership and 21 Irrefutable Laws of Leadership**

Chapter Ten

Self-help sections of bookshops, libraries and online stores conjured up the same image of the dating agencies I joined in the early 1990s.

Desperation.

While trying to find the courage to step into the self-help section of WH Smith, I was purchasing books for my daughter as a way to apologise for not being the good father I should have been. She had progressed from Roald Dahl and was now enjoying the thrills of J.K. Rowling with the wonderful Harry Potter books.

Too embarrassed to go into the self-help section of the bookstore, I went to the magazine section to read Empire, a movie magazine I had been enjoying since 1991. En route, something caught my eye.

A magazine called SUCCESS – the headline read something like "How to improve your life."

Just what I was looking for – the signal. The sign. The knowledge that a higher being was looking out for me.

Sometimes when we're lost, God provides clues and hints. We usually miss what they are, although in this case, it was obvious. Inside the magazine included topics such as:

- Being the best you can be.
- Lose weight.
- Be your own boss.
- How to overcome doubt.
- Have an attitude for gratitude.

There was so much insight and value. Amazing people such as Jack Canfield, John Maxwell, Jim Rohn, Darren Hardy, Tony Robbins, Brandon Burchard, people who years later would become my heroes.

Shweta kindly arranged a magazine subscription and several years later, I'm still an avid reader and have studied hundreds of books and audio CDs from the contributors, guest writers and cover stars.

SUCCESS contains my favourite all-time quotes and back then it was eye-opening. I had never heard anyone talk like this:

- You are 100% responsible for your life.

- Giving is living.

- If you want more, you have to become more.

I had always blamed others, it's so easy to. I never realised that it was all up to me.

Giving is living encourages you to donate 10% of your income to good causes.

10%!!!!!

That sounds like a lot, especially when you're paying income tax, national insurance, rent, food, travel, babysitting and a whole array of insurances every month.

Giving is living was about putting other people's needs above your own. That is something I didn't do enough of, so decided to give it a try.

Being a parent, I made a donation to Save The Children. Something happened that's hard to describe, it was like my soul started to heal. I started feeling like I was a good person for making a difference. Having spent years suffering from depression, I also arranged monthly donations to The Samarians. Comic Relief had always been part of my childhood so it was natural to support them.

Sponsoring friends on Justgiving for marathons, mountain climbs and bike rides was also done every month. I then progressed to participating as well as fundraising like taking part in walks for Marie Curie Cancer Care, jumping out of an airplane for Alec's Angels and becoming volunteer chairman for Informa's Prince's Trust charity. Then something amazing happened.

LESSON 15 - PERSONAL DEVELOPMENT WILL OPEN YOUR EYES TO A NEW WORLD.

Your levels of energy and wellbeing go through the roof. Positive attitude, taking 100% responsibility and the karma I experienced from giving to others meant that companies I had been chasing for months started contacting me for interviews.

Giving makes the world place a better place and it's a way of thanking God for all he has done. If you wait until you are rich to give to others, you will never be rich.

In terms of becoming more, here's what I did:

a) Read 30 minutes every day on self-improvement.

b) Went to the gym three times a week to lose weight and get in shape.

c) Started praying every day, not out of desperation, but to express my gratitude to God for the new life he had given me and the amazing family who had supported me through this tough time.

d) Woke up at 5.30 am instead of 6.30am. Successful people start early, get more done and have fewer distractions.

e) Stopped wasting my time on watching the news or gossip.

f) Spent 10 minutes every night writing in a gratitude journal. This helped me sleep better. Research also shows that writing what you're grateful for every day helps reduce stress and depression.

It takes time to rebuild confidence once it has been shattered. As my confidence soared and I opened my eyes to a new world... companies wanted to meet me because my anger had gone and been replaced with positivity... then they started to give me job offers.

I accepted a role as a sales manager at a huge company which alternated between the impressive FTSE 250 and the elusive FTSE 100 on the London Stock Exchange.

RECAP

- You are 100% responsible for your life.
- Giving is living.
- If you want more, you have to become more.
- Work harder on yourself than you do at your job.

- Avoid news and gossip, especially first thing in the morning.

"Investing in yourself is the best investment you will ever make. It will not only improve your life, it will improve the lives of all those around you." – **Robin Sharma, author The Leader Who Had No Title and The Monk Who Sold His Ferrari**

"Be the change you want to see in the world." – **Mahatma Gandhi**

Chapter Eleven

Informa PLC had 7,000 staff and generated over £200,000,000 a year in profit. I joined the shipping division in early 2011. The shipping industry had been traumatised by the recession between 2008 and 2010.

The effects of the world economy can be seen through the eyes of shipping:

1. When people spend less money, fewer products are put in shipping containers to be sent around the world to different countries.

2. Ships make less money since they're transporting less containers.

3. Ports import fewer goods and make less money.

4. There's a massive supply chain that hurts along the way from van drivers to trains to warehouses.

5. Loss of money means less profit for companies.

6. Less profit for companies means less money paid in tax to government which leads to cuts in public spending.

7. Less profit for companies nearly always leads to job losses.

90% of world trade is carried by ship. The chairs you sit on, light bulbs you switch on when you walk into your home or office, TVs you watch, iPhones you watch, clothes you wear, furniture you sit on, watches you wear. All arrive from around the world in ships.

I was hired to generate a whopping 20% growth for the shipping division, so not only did I have to deal with the aftermath of the shipping recession, but also a worldwide recession which had caused advertising to be cut everywhere.

Armed with a slight increase in salary, I inherited two staff.

Grayson, an aging yet super-fit triathlete who had been in the business for 15 years. He knew everyone and had spent his life taking incoming calls. As a result, when times got tough, he couldn't sell. In one meeting, he actually handed over a sheet of paper to a client and said "read this list of features I have typed up, it's why you should do business with us."

Kingsley was tall, athletic, handsome, young and Mr. Popular in the office. He had six months of success and thought he was untouchable as a sales person. If you think you're the best and you stop growing, there's always trouble ahead.

So, I was managing staff who didn't want to be managed, who resented having a boss and hated being told what to do.

In addition, I had my own sales target, so the pressure was on. Informa often appears on lists of the best companies to work for in terms of the benefits offered. They did four things which were brilliant:

- They sent me on sales courses which made me improve every day.
- They sent me on management courses which helped me become a better manager.
- They gave me a corporate credit card and iPhone which made me feel like a grown-up.
- My boss, Fergus, offered weekly 1-2-1- meetings and fortnightly mentoring sessions.

I've never had mentoring before and strongly recommend it to everyone. Fergus was someone of value I could discuss my career with. He gave advice, listened and recommended good books to read.

Mentoring gives you the confidence to believe in yourself. Mentoring offers you the right direction instead of wasting time travelling down the wrong paths which unfortunately, so many people do. Mentoring gives you hope, and hope is what so many of us need. Mentoring guides you towards success.

Successful people get mentored. Richard Branson was mentored by Sir Freddie Laker. Oprah Winfrey was mentored by Maya Angelou. Mark Zuckerberg was mentored by Steve Jobs. Quincy Jones, who produced Michael Jackson's Thriller was mentored by Ray Charles.

These inspirational people have said that they would never have had as much success if they'd never had a mentor.

LESSON 16 - GETTING A MENTOR WILL ACCELERERATE YOUR CAREER.

Fergus was four years younger than me, yet was at an executive level in his early thirties and had three kids. He was one of life's super achievers. Despite his success, he always treated me with respect and we became a powerful team.

Through my own desire to improve, to thank Informa for the support they had given me, plus working with Fergus who offered mentoring, here's what happened:

I got introduced to many like-minded people on my career path.

I met senior executives in the business who were supportive and kind.

Rather than just giving 10% to charity, I started doing my own fundraising as well.

My working hours increased from nine hours a day to twelve hours a day.

I enjoyed going to work every day.

I made my boss look good.

I contributed towards an increase in profits for Informa's shipping division.

When management are happy, new opportunities often open up and I was given the chance to launch a new event, the Containerisation International Awards. Success attracts success and for a while, life was promising.

RECAP

- Find a mentor.
- Respect their time.
- Be open to learning.

"A mentor is someone who allows you to see the hope inside yourself."
– Oprah Winfrey

"A mentor is someone who sees more talent and ability within you, than you see in yourself, and helps bring it out of you." – **Bob Proctor, author, The ABCs of Success and The Art of Living**

Chapter Twelve

Launching a new event in 6 months is possible if you don't sleep much and have no life. That's what happened.

Personal Development expert Jim Rohn once said "*Become* a *millionaire, not* for the *money*, but for what it *will make* of *you* to achieve it." It related back to an earlier quote "if you want to have more, you need to become more."

That's how I treated this event, it wasn't about getting another target and bonus – although that helped. Informa had tried to launch the Containerisation International Awards over the years and it hadn't worked. An event launch also takes 9-12 months:

a)   The odds were stacked against me.

b)   It had failed many times before.

c)   Many colleagues wanted me to fail – when you become successful, you attract a lot of haters, even when you've never done or said a single bad thing towards them.

When I asked Fergus for advice, his response was simple: "Get on a plane, look people in the white of their eyes and talk to them. You can do this, I believe in you." That's another thing mentors do, help you believe you can achieve anything.

Having always done business in the UK, for the first time, I was flying across the world, meeting customers in a monumental effort to win back their business by getting them to sponsor our awards and advertise in our magazine and website.

USA was a tough market to break into. We had gone from 60% market share when there was little competition in 2008 to 10% market share in 2011 when budgets had been reduced and more competitors popped up and worked from home – that meant they charged less money and being small, offered better service than a large corporation.

When you make the effort to travel to the west coast USA, customers appreciate it and give you more time. From where I live in England, it took me three trains to get to Heathrow, then an 11 hour and 30-minute flight to Los Angeles, then an hour by taxi along endless highways and heavy traffic. That's 15 hours to see a customer!

Also, I wasn't like every sales person just asking for money. I thoroughly researched everyone I met on LinkedIn, spent hours studying their websites to learn about their offering, took insight from the editorial team to share with every company I met and asked questions to show that I genuinely cared.

Port of Los Angeles and Port of Long Beach, the two biggest ports in USA and the top 20 ports in the world were absolute behemoths, with shipping containers stacked high and lasting for miles. After the meeting, they kindly told me it was refreshing to meet someone who had done their homework, offered value and didn't try so hard close the deal.

A two-hour flight later, Port of Seattle followed. Seattle is a lot like London. Cold, rainy, with great coffee houses. I went to the original Starbucks and enjoyed the eclectic markets. Peter McGraw, head of real estate and marketing at Port of Seattle, was a great host, a talented music producer in his free time and someone I would become friends with over the years.

I then headed to Europe, to meet Port of Rotterdam, the biggest port in Europe, then Port of Hamburg, the second biggest in Europe and Port of Antwerp, the third biggest port in Europe. I slept on planes and in taxis. Ate whatever I could grab which was rarely healthy.

Overall, I generated over £350,000 from my travels in a year.

With the internet, we can do business with anyone in the world – and that's pretty amazing – but it has its limits.

The internet connects us all, but it doesn't really "connect" us on a business level.

Connection is shaking someone's hand, looking them in the eye while you speak, having drinks, eating a client's local cuisine and appreciating the flavours and smell, respecting and experiencing the culture, appreciating an iconic building - you can't do this sitting behind a computer.

I love the internet, but nothing can match the experience of travelling and meeting people. You learn a lot by travelling.

LESSON 17 – TRAVEL AS MUCH AS YOU CAN.

USA

Everything was so big. Apart from New York, public transport is a pain, so you have to drive everywhere for hours. We're so lucky in the UK to have the transport services we have. Ignore most of what you read about Americans, they're not obsessed with money, they're not all mid-westerners supporting Trump and they're not all gun-raving nuts. They're a welcoming nation with spectacular national parks and they enjoy meeting people from different cultures, especially the UK.

Canada

Every cliché about Canada is true. They're lovely, kind, happy people. Tim Horton's coffee is better than anything Starbucks produces and doing business with them is always an absolute joy.

Germany

I've spent more time here than anywhere in Europe. Germans are straight talkers, no nonsense. When they have a few beers, they open up and tell great jokes. The Vietnamese part of Hamburg serves the best food. As you would expect, everything runs efficiently.

Spain

Wonderful people. Treat you like family. They had less money to spend on advertising and fought over every Euro, however, a pleasure to work with, especially Port of Barcelona.

Netherlands

Everyone is tall and beautiful. A bike-friendly city. Great to walk around Amsterdam. The Dutch always made me feel welcome. Port of Amsterdam became one of my best clients.

Belgium

Antwerp city centre is crammed with traffic. Waffles and beer are delicious.

Chocolates are incredible. Smallest airport I've ever seen. You have to fly by propeller plane which is a terrifying flight full of bumps, jumps and shaking.

Japan

You can be animated with Americans and Canadians, not with the Japanese who prefer more conservative people. Never attempt to hard sell or you will scare them off. Most business is done through a middleman since the elders rarely speak English.

South Korea

People are amazing and becoming more westernised. Karaoke bars are where all the business transactions take place. South Koreans have a terrific sense of humour and are also wonderful hosts that will treat you like family.

China

One of the fastest growing nations on earth, yet people rarely answer the phone and hardly anyone has voice mail. They negotiate quickly without caring that much about value. Everyone has a western name on email and they take 6-9 months to pay invoices. Primarily male-driven and like the Japanese, nobody questions authority.

Middle East

It's like doing business in Hollywood. They act like your best friend, insist they'd love to work with you, then you don't hear from them. Nobody ever admits they're wrong. They call it "saving face." They like big hotels, big money and the men talk a big talk. The English people here are easy to work with and enjoy sharing stories about living in a different world.

Czech Republic

Some people make jokes, however, you can't tell from their faces if they're happy. That's the Czech people. They're friendly once you talk to them. Apart from top hotels and restaurants, not that many people speak English. Prague is a fantastic city for walking. I've seen more Italian restaurants here than anywhere outside Italy.

Italy

Most Italians I've worked with are happy to open a bottle of wine for a 9am meeting. Like the French, having wine, cheese and pastries seems to have no effect on their diet, and the Italians also have pasta and pizza. A warm welcome always awaits you.

France

Never attempt to speak French unless you are fluent. They will look at you like you're an alien. There's always been a rivalry between France and England over who has the better wine (France) food (England) style (French) culture (British) and football team (debatable). These differences should bring us together, but they don't. A tough place to do business so I recommend always trying to partner with a French person or French company and then trying to sell to them.

If you want to do business around the world, get out of your office and go meet people.

Study several phrases in every language, simple ones like "How are you" "I'm fine, thanks" Where is the toilet?" and "Your beer is better than the Americans". That one is a favourite everywhere you travel. In certain countries there are customs you must abide by. Bowing in Asia is vital. Getting taken out every night is common and you don't say no. With the Chinese, never ask what you're eating, you will always be shocked.

Learning basic phrases takes about 30 minutes per day for a week and shows mutual respect.

My family were also enjoying the rewards from my travel:

a)   Overdraft gone.

b)   Bank loans gone.

c)   We took an amazing family holiday to Disneyworld.

d)   We donated thousands of pounds every year to good causes.

e)   We missed each other more and that brought us closer together.

RECAP

- Travelling outside your country opens your mind to new possibilities.
- Travelling helps you learn and appreciate more about the world.
- Potential clients will always give you more time when you travel long distances to see them. That increases your chances of doing business.
- Learn several basic phrases in every language before travelling.

"One doesn't discover new land without consenting to lose sight, for a very long time, of the shore." **– Andrew Gide –author and Nobel Prize winner in Literature**

Chapter Thirteen

Managing a team is like managing a teenager and my heart goes out to every parent and especially to every teacher who has to deal with teens on a daily basis.

Every parent has warned me of the horrors of raising a teenager.

I was convinced that would never happen to me since my daughter, Shreya, is an angel. Quiet, hard-working, polite, a straight A student, my bond with her was special. Since my wife's salon was fully booked on Saturdays, I would take Shreya to the library, movies, friend's parties and lunch. She was my best friend and she also helped me reconnect with my father.

Then she became a teenager – and EVERYTHING changed.

Growing up, my father worked all the time. As a result, he was often short-tempered and frustrated by life. When your child cries in the night because of a cold, after you wake up to take care of them, you don't fall asleep immediately. Instead you go into work the next day exhausted and unable to concentrate. That takes its toll. Working overtime to provide for your family, I understand now why Dad missed so many events and was frustrated so easily. It made me appreciate all the sacrifices my incredible parents had made, even more so when my father was awarded an MBE at Buckingham Palace for his dedication to the NHS and his charity work.

As Shreya approached 13, she started behaving like my team.

- Not listening.
- Promising to do things and not doing them.
- Not appreciating all I do.
- Failing to understand that everything I do, I do for them.
- Criticising me behind my back for being too serious.
- Making me lose my temper.
- Generally pissing me off.

In my heart, I still loved my daughter. Couldn't say the same about the staff I inherited.

Being a parent is an incredible learning experience - and anyone who is a parent to a healthy child doesn't realise how lucky they are, having met many people who have either sick children or who are unable to have kids.

No matter how many blogs, articles and books you read, nothing can prepare you for a teenager. Seeing your angel become a monster is traumatic and the fights were getting so intense, it was affecting my marriage to Shweta. I was so scared of getting back into depression and screwing everything up again.

I couldn't go back to that dark place, I refused to.

LESSON 18 - DEALING WITH DIFFICULT PEOPLE

Here's what I did to deal with difficult colleagues at work. This is not just useful for managing staff, it's for the colleagues you work with who get their kicks from being annoying, never turning up to work on time, blaming others, making excuses and never being there when you need them.

Listen

- Why are they angry?
- Are they aware of their tone?
- What is their body language like?

Often you have to kindly ask a few times what is wrong. The first response is usually "nothing." Anthony Iannarino, author, speaker and sales leader, gives valuable advice on this: "When you finish asking a question and want to hear more, pause and count silently for four seconds... quite often they will start talking." People hate silences. It's often then you discover more.

Ask what is important to them in life

Again, it shows you care. What matters to them? I had a colleague who was always rude to everyone. Turns out her mother had cancer, but people always wanted things from her and never asked how she was, so she replied with blunt force. Listening to her vent made for a better working relationship.

Don't Tell Them What To Do

This is one of the most difficult things to implement. When someone doesn't listen, all you want to do is lecture them. They need to realise themselves that they have to change.

Don't lose your temper

This is obvious, yet very hard to do. Use Mel Robbins Five Second Rule. Count backwards from 5...4...3...2...1... and then react. Same goes for a client deal when they take their business elsewhere. Count to five and walk it off. Being confrontational is a natural reaction, yet rarely achieves anything.

Protection

When things get serious, have a member of Human Resources or a manager in the room as a witness. When people have stuff going on they can't express, fists can fly and often words are uttered which cannot be taken back.

The results

Kingsley's behaviour was insecurity. He didn't like me being number one, when he used to be the best. I assured him we were working together as a team and I was there to support him. He was also a dad and a fellow Arsenal fan, which helped us connect on a deeper level. We ended up going on business trips together and he did well for himself over the next year. But sometimes... things just don't work out.

Grayson went from bad to worse. His backstabbing, laziness and the constant lies made life hell. There's an old saying "hire for attitude, train for skills." Grayson had neither. He had been lucky in a business where being the most senior, he had taken incoming calls for years and managed the biggest accounts.

Magazines don't have the power they once had, so Grayson had to pick up the phone and call people, which he struggled to do. Maybe 10 calls a day. If you can't make 30 calls a day selling your product, how do you succeed?

We went through the usual processes – a Performance Improvement Plan where he promised to improve and didn't. Then Human Resources got involved. It was a painful, long, tedious process that took a lot of paperwork and tested my patience. I kicked out someone who was well connected and it made clients dislike me.

A young kid called Alan Hart replaced him. He was softly spoken, genuine and dreamed of going travelling to Australia. We worked on his goals and dreams as part of his sales target. Two years later, he achieved that when he travelled to Australia with his family.

That's what happens when staff have the right attitude and have a manager who cares – they get positive results.

RECAP

- Ask what's wrong and pause. People will often fill in the gaps.
- Don't tell people what to do.
- Listen.

"When dealing with people, remember you are not dealing with creatures of logic, but with creatures of emotion, creatures bristling with prejudice, and motivated by pride and vanity." – **Dale Carnegie, author, How To Win Friends and Influence People**

"Be kind, for everyone you meet is fighting a hard battle."

– Anon

Chapter Fourteen

For every win, there should be a reward. I'm not taking about a holiday or Michelin star restaurant, although that's nice if you can afford it. Going to the movies, buying a new outfit, eating out at a restaurant or having a long weekend are wonderful rewards.

Celebrating the wins gives you confidence and power to push forward and that helps when it comes to the losses.

When I was the top salesperson in my division in 2011, 2012 and 2013, my basic salary went by 20% and commission was doubled.

Working in sales won't make you a millionaire, however, when you do well, it allows you to lead a decent lifestyle and take care of those around you.

Despite the wins, I never gave up. I kept pushing myself to see how far I could get. That's what greatness is all about. Seeing how far you can go, while still taking care of those around you.

Winning the CSO Club was the ultimate prize.

I'm always disappointed that it's only sales people who get these rewards. Although we deal with rejection more than most people, much of our success is thanks to talented journalists, production, support staff, HR and work colleagues. Companies should consider rewarding everyone who makes a valuable contribution, not just those who generate revenue.

At Informa, the Top Gun of sales people were given the holiday of a lifetime to take a partner on an all-expenses paid trip to a heavenly destination. The best was St Lucia.

Close your eyes and imagine golden sands, stunning blue seas, fresh air, hot weather, world-class customer service and mouth-watering fresh food.

Le Body Holiday Resort normally costed £10,000 for a couple. That doesn't include flights or spending money.

Even though this had been earned, it was still an absolute honour and I'll always be grateful for this opportunity from Informa - taking my wife on a world-class holiday was good for our marriage and spending quality time with like-minded and wonderful people makes life more enjoyable.

Account manager, James Epstein, a loveable big bear who went on to become one of my best friends, brought along his sweet girlfriend Ilana. Laura Stanham, an awesome sales person with a northern twang brought Gemma Stanham, her equally mad and fun sister. Jan Chowdhury, one of the happiest people I ever met and the first Muslim I ever hung out with, was a leader in the pharma division. Fred Urban an eccentric German who was well travelled, mastered government contracts. Maxwell Harvey, ladies' man and master of closing and storytelling. John Purkis, a young divisional director who looked like a member of One Direction, yet was always welcoming. Alex Wilkinson, an exceptional grafter and all-around nice guy. Mike Ellicott, a successful sales manager who was dating the fabulous Nikki Handley.

Over the years I have turned to many of them for advice on business, support on a marketing campaign, friendship when a loved one passed away or advice on hiring a member of staff - and they've never let me down.

LESSON 19 - CELEBRATE YOUR SUCCESS, EVEN THE SMALL ONES, THEN AIM FOR MORE SUCCESS.

Too many times corporate London gets painted as white male, yet here we were - strength in diversity of people, religion, culture, sex and sexuality - it was heart-warming. One of those moments in life you never forget.

When times get hard, which they always will, it's people like this who will support you, encourage you and push you to be the best. Some call them account buddies. Others call them inner circle. Either way, they're vital to your success.

Because as much as you plan your career and stick to your goals, there's always going to be shocks – and the biggest ones were yet to come.

RECAP

- Celebrate wins.
- Celebrate progress.
- Have an attitude of gratitude.

"Celebrate your successes. Find some humour in your failures." – **Sam Walton, founder Walmart**

"It's important to celebrate any victory in life." – **Jillian Michaels, personal trainer, TV personality**

Chapter Fifteen

Lindsey Roberts was one of the few female CEOs running a FTSE 100 company in the UK. Despite the unfair criticism women in power attract - which has little to do with their character and more to do with their gender - Lindsey was a visionary.

She was unlike any CEO I had ever met.

a) No fancy clothes.

b) Straight talking.

c) The odd profanity here and there.

d) The kind of person you could enjoy a beer with.

e) She inspired others.

f) Lindsey supported my career and the charity work I had taken on board from walks for Marie Curie Cancer Care, growing an embarrassing moustache every year for Movember and raising money and awareness when I became chairman of Informa's Prince's Trust charity.

When a new CEO Carter joined, Lindsey disappeared; no email, no thank you, nothing.

I don't know what happened, although I'm disappointed I never had the chance to share a farewell drink with the best CEO I ever worked with.

When a new CEO joins a business, they stamp their authority with their own vision and executive team.

Carter got rid of my people at Informa such as Fotini Liontou, a remarkable head of content who was also managing triplets at home. Nicola Whyke, an excellent publisher with a wicked sense of humour, Sarah Walker, an intelligent business director, Jen Trevena, analyst extraordinaire.

Carter also did something I considered unthinkable. He got rid of the learning and development team to save money. Again, another team of fabulous women were gone.

Learning and development is the lifeblood of a company. It helps staff rise through the ranks quicker. It's how experienced and successful managers continue to improve. Informa generated £900,000,000 a year with £200,000,000 in profits so it's not like they were struggling.

The learning and development team cost approx. £150,000 a year on staff and another £100,000 invested on venue hire for training. (training should always take place away from the office so you can focus and not be dragged into internal meetings). In return, the people they trained like me delivered millions of pounds of extra advertising and sponsorship revenue.

I appreciate it's easy to criticise someone when you haven't walked in their shoes and they haven't explained clearly why they made the decision, but this made no sense.

Once they cut the learning department, sales revenue went down. They blamed the drop in ad revenue on market conditions, decline in print, then Brexit.

No business with any self-respect blames the recession. Winners take responsibility. People with an inability to lead blame the recession.

Informa lost its heart and became a place of hitting targets. The great culture disappeared. I had no idea who the new MD was now since she never said hello, Lara something or another. A good leader like a Richard Branson, Bill McDermott of SAP, Jack Welch of General Motors or a John Maxwell – they walk the floor – in other words, they talk to people who are not just executives. They inspire staff, not with emails, but by shaking hands, asking how they are doing, inspiring.

I don't recall any of Carter's team ever doing this with me or any of my colleagues.

Businesses don't have to be cold places where it's only about profits. They can also have leaders who inspire and show that they care for others.

Informa is a Business to Business media company everyone likes to have on their CV much like Haymarket, Centaur, EMAP, Future

Publishing, UBM, so they knew people would keep applying for jobs, regardless of how they treated others.

Through all the chaos, Fergus got a promotion to head of marketing services (head of sales) when they combined shipping, pharmacy and insurance teams. Fergus had always spoken about me eventually being the head of Lloyd's List shipping sales, in other words, his deputy. I had proved myself by smashing targets, achieving success and doing wonders for Corporate Social Responsibility with my charity work. This would be a huge promotion and take me on the road to a director.

I prepared for the role, spent weeks on my presentation which had been in my mind for years to justify why I was the right person. I knew Fergus would be my biggest advocate.

Instead, he gave the role to his friend, Dom which was a massive disappointment.

Dom had a reputation for telling awful jokes, being unreasonable, taking credit for other peoples' success and disappearing when times got tough. Unfortunately, the rumours were true.

He behaved like Donald Trump:

• Picking fights with everyone.

• Taking joy from humiliating people.

• Behaving like an unprincipled bully.

As a manager, you don't have to be liked, but you do need to be respected. Dom was neither. It always surprises me how many people get promoted, not because they are qualified, but because they are mates with someone.

Fergus no longer had 1-2-1s or mentoring and distanced himself from me. When I asked why, he said he was busy and Dom would take care of that.

Dom never did any personal development, no mentoring or ever said anything to inspire. All the class, understanding and support I had from Fergus disappeared the day Dom was appointed. He ran the division on fear:

- Do this or lose your job.
- Do this or you will be replaced.
- Do this or you will be a massive disappointment to yourself.

How many of us have had to deal with awful managers like this?

If that wasn't bad enough, Dom did the dumbest thing I have ever seen a manager do to a colleague who was successful.

He took away most of my clients and gave them to young sales people with little experience to show who was boss.

Who takes away business from a top member of staff and gives it to people with little experience?

I warned him this was a terrible strategic move. I warned him this would lead to a loss in revenue. I warned him our confidence would be destroyed. He didn't listen and as a result:

- The team missed its target.
- We lost commission.
- We struggled to pay the bills.
- Life was a living hell every day at work.

Like a coward, Dom blamed everyone except himself and made life a nightmare for everyone around him...

LESSON 20 - ADAPT TO CHANGE.

I didn't deal with this well. Imagine you have been living a good life, then someone comes along and takes it from you.

Going to a job every day that you hate is an unbearable experience and one that many of us have all had to endure.

- You feel sick as your immunity systems slows down.
- Insomnia kicks in.
- You become worse at your job because you stop caring.
- It starts affecting your home life.

- Depression kicks in – no matter your age or gender, depression is a killer. According to government statistics, 17 million days were lost last year due to depression. That's a whopping £2,700,000 the British economy lost.

- Panic attacks become more common. Instead of working as a team and serving clients, we all wondered how someone as crass and rude as Dom could get a job in management.

Dom was sneaky. He never had meetings with us in a group, only 1-2-1, so it was always his word against ours. Nobody wants to lose their job and when someone more powerful than you has the potential to fire you because they're an idiot, you tend to listen to what they say...

... especially when you have a mortgage and a family.

I should have had the confidence to fight back. Instead, it destroyed my self-worth. When my mother was taken to hospital in 2015 due to complications with her colostomy bag, she was on life support for two weeks.

Seeing your mother unable to communicate, speak, or move was traumatising. Not once did Dom ask how she was, how she was feeling or how I was coping. That's the kind of manager he was.

With our whole family struggling, my confidence faded. I became vulnerable. That's when bullies attack.

They threaten, curse, put you down, take advantage and you don't have the strength to fight back. Other examples of what Dom did:

- Continually tell me I was an embarrassment if I failed to hit target.

- Advised me to stop caring for people, because it was a waste of time

- Arranged meetings and didn't turn up.

- Went away on business for a week and didn't tell his staff.

- Went away on business to places like South America where we made £40,000 a year and brought back zero business.

- Took 20-25 sick days off work.

- Promised to call certain clients and never did. This lost us our biggest account, worth over £100,000 because he didn't call them when he claimed he did.

- Destroyed client relationships we spent years building and handed over to people with little to no experience. This caused the business to lose money every month.

- We missed targets, therefore we missed commission and struggled financially.

- Launched a magazine in 2015 at a time when magazines were going downhill and everybody was reading the news online.

- He was an appalling salesman – this is an example of what happened.

I secured a meeting with a director of ARUP, one of the top businesses in the UK. Dom advised me to say this "I am an oily salesman. My job is to get my grubby hands on your budget."

He claimed he started every meeting like this to ease the customer. Talk about embarrassing.

At the end of the meeting, which was simply a getting-to-know-you, Dom asked where he should send the contract to be signed.

ARUP'S director became awkward and told him to take it easy. He didn't take my call for 3 weeks since he clearly didn't want to do business with someone like Dom.

The list goes on and on. When we made a complaint to human resources, they told us to speak with Fergus. I was confident my former mentor would be supportive and understanding of his staff having to deal with a boss who was mentally unstable.

Instead Fergus was livid and demand that we concentrate on hitting target. I couldn't believe it. He stopped caring.

When a member of staff complains about bullying, you never ever ignore it and tell them to focus on hitting target. You assure them you will look into it immediately.

I tried to reason with Fergus, but he was adamant Dom knew what he was doing, even though everyone else considered him incompetent and dishonest.

Fergus was an overachiever and had done well for somebody so young. That created resentment among many people, who criticised him unfairly. I always stood by Fergus when staff talked behind his back. I didn't care if it made me unpopular, loyalty is a valuable asset. I put in the extra hours and Fergus became my first mentor and the first boss I thought was truly amazing.

And this was how it ended. Being stabbed in the back and hurt by someone I truly admired.

You know the old saying "people don't leave companies, they leave bad bosses", that's never been truer.

Change is inevitable.

It may not be necessary and it may not always be fair, but it will happen. You shouldn't fear change, since you don't grow doing the same thing every day. At the same time, you mustn't let it destroy your self-worth.

RECAP

- Change is inevitable.
- Change happens for a reason.
- Learn to adapt through difficult times.

"Those who cannot change their minds cannot change anything." – **George Bernard Shaw, critic, author of Pygmalion**

"There is nothing wrong with change, if it's in the right direction." – **Winston Churchill**

Chapter Sixteen

The bullying and aggression from Dom meant that every day I wanted to quit. Nobody wants to leave a job where they achieved success and made good friends. Dom then insisted he accompany me on business trips across Europe. This sometimes happens with first time or struggling staff, yes. With experienced staff, this was unusual. So, I asked why?

"To keep an eye on you" was his weird reply.

"I'm not having you follow me around Europe for a week." It was creepy. It was harassment.

He promised me this was happening with all my colleagues – since nobody trusted Dom, I called my colleagues and they had no knowledge of this.

That was the final straw. I resigned from Informa without a job to go to.

Making decisions when you're angry is never a smart thing to do. I emailed the head of Human Resources, a hardworking and talented woman called Michelle Carr who was never appreciated enough for what she did. I also forwarded my resignation letter onto my four sales colleagues.

I made a list of all the problems with Dom, paying particular attention how young Alan Hart in his twenties with little sales experience was bringing back £40,000 a year from South America, yet Dom went there and brought back nothing, making our business lose more money.

At Informa, you have to endure rigorous paperwork before going on business.

a)   How much money you are spending on the business trip?

b)   How much business you will bring back?

c)   You are held accountable to that.

Dom brought back nothing and got away with it. He had caused the division to miss target 12 months in a row! He told lies and alienated not only his team but the events team with his rudeness. It felt so good to let out these frustrations in writing.

What happened next was a mega shit-storm:

- HR passed the email onto the sales and marketing director of Informa and CEO of Lloyd's List.

- My team members were cheering at how I put Dom in his place.

- One of my colleagues stupidly forwarded my email to Fergus.

- Fergus berated me for destroying the team dynamic. I respectfully disagreed and told Fergus this was partly his fault for not dealing with the Dom problem when so many people had complained about him.

- Dom got demoted from managing 10 members of staff to managing the only person he ever cared about – himself.

- My work colleagues congratulated me for teaching a bully a lesson.

Goodness had won. The bully had been defeated.

I read a transcript of a talk Bill Clinton gave in Silicon Valley a few years ago. To paraphrase: "people in the future business get rewarded. People in the today business fail."

Magazines are not the future. Technology is: AI, virtual reality, self-driving cars, cryptocurrency, drones, plus the internet will continue to grow and develop.

I was so desperate to find work I called in favours from recruitment consultants I had helped out over the years. They had several clients who were interested in offering me a job. Instead of working for another big, complex corporation, my colleague Maxwell advised I work for a small or medium-sized business since they had many advantages.

No corporate politics, you can speak directly to those in charge and I'd rise up the chain faster. It sounded like a good plan.

Unfortunately, the more senior roles you apply for, the more they demand experience in that sector. The only companies that wanted to meet me were magazines and as we know, they were not the future.

What choice did I have? I resigned from a bullying boss. After the millions of pounds I had generated from Informa, I thought they would fight for me to stay. Sadly, they completely failed to recognise my worth.

I had an interview, followed by a presentation I put together for a small business in Chelsea Harbour, an unusual part of London - a harbour full of yachts surrounded by multi-million pound flats owned by the Russians and Middle-Eastern millionaires that are empty most of the year. In the summer, the place was packed with the super-rich who flew to England to enjoy a few days of sunshine.

Publishing Director, Ian, was a nice bloke and had 20 years' experience as a director of big businesses. Here's why I accepted a job with him.

- The office was quiet.

- They wanted someone to turn around their struggling magazines and they told me I could do it.

- The previous sales team left for different reasons that had nothing to do with management.

- I would hire a new sales team to suit my needs.

- I was promised the awful magazine website could be redeveloped into something all-singing, all-dancing.

- I was told it was a family environment where everyone got along.

4 months later, this is what the reality was:

- The office was quiet because most people didn't want to be there.

- The reason the previous sales team left was they were fiddling online advertising statistics before giving them to clients, especially our biggest client, who spent over £40,000 a year. Sadly, many sales people do this to ensure they earn commission. Never lie, you always get caught.

- I only had a £30,000 salary to hire great salespeople, which is not enough. Good people in London cost £35,000 a year. Great people in London are over £40,000 a year.

- You pay pennies, you get muppets.

- The awful magazine website wasn't redeveloped.

- It was not a family environment, it was a work environment.

- Dom struck again.

After the humiliation of being demoted at Informa, nobody heard from Dom. Colleagues were happier. Life was good without him.

Then Dom sent a deeply offensive email to Ian and also the deputy director. It was sent anonymously, although every single word Dom used had been uttered by him. It was his language. His tone. He claimed I was a failure, that I was terrible at my Informa job, was under investigation for corruption and would destroy the current business I was working for.

If you have ever been stalked or harassed, you will know exactly how awful this intrusion feels.

LESSON 21: DEALING WITH FAILURE.

Lies. Lies and utter lies! I understand why Dom behaved this way - his career was finished. He had been humiliated at Informa although that was 100% his fault: he chose to bully others, he chose to be mean and he choose to lie to everyone around him.

A real man would take responsibility for his actions. Dom was a bully and bullies are cowards so he learned nothing. I felt sorry for his wife who knew nothing about his abusive behaviour.

I passed this email onto my colleagues at Informa, their reaction was one of horror and every single person knew Dom had done this.

I expected full support. Instead my new company's HR manager went into a mass panic. Why?

Despite giving her three quality job references, she didn't bother to contact them. Who hires people without a reference?

Clearly this new company I was working for. So instead of sympathising with me regarding the online abuse and dishonesty I was dealing with, the HR Manager contacted my references, asking the most stupid questions with the following:

"To satisfy our reference query, within the context of this unusual situation, an honest and accurate response to the questions below would be most appreciated:

- Dates of employment within your team or organisation?
- Job roles while employed at Informa, including the final job title before departure?
- How many direct reports did Niraj have?
- Professional and/or personal achievement whilst working with you?
- General approach to clients and colleagues?
- Any outstanding disciplinary issues at the time of departure?
- Any live disciplinary actions on file for Niraj?
- Sales achievements in the last 2 years?
- Any customer complaints in the past 2 years?"

I've reviewed many job references when staff are hired and I've written many references for other people. Never have I seen or heard of anyone ask such crass questions.

The HR Manager was trying to cover her own back for failing to do her job. Nobody in management asked me how I was or how I was coping. Instead I came under intense scrutiny.

I contacted one of the top employment lawyers in London who worked at Olswang solicitors. He told me I could take legal action, get an injunction against Microsoft to release the details of the person who sent the email from the anonymous Outlook address.

It could drag on for months, cost me anywhere from £8,000 – 10,000 of legal fees and for all my trouble, all I would get was an apology from a manager who bullied me.

I respect my money too much to waste £10,000, so I complained to Informa CEO Carter who passed it onto his team.

- Dom was investigated.

- Many people were questioned.

- It made Dom look incredibly stupid.

- Everyone knew he did it.

- Nobody could prove it.

- He got away with abuse and bullying.

It was sickening. Anytime a bully torments another human being and gets away with it, it makes your blood boil.

With the HR Manager's gross inefficiency and management's lack of support, I then realised that I had made a mistake joining them.

The grass is always greener on the other side. This one had shades of blue.

When you have a mortgage and family responsibilities, people have a dangerous tendency to settle for less than what they deserve. I'm an optimist and believed management would change and support me.

I was wrong.

After Ian got unfairly booted out for "early retirement" without notice or saying goodbye, the weird bearded Deputy Director got promoted to CEO and started playing God. Many people in the office were nervous and would ask me for advice. When I spoke to the CEO he made his stance very clear.

He didn't care. He simply wanted targets hit and refused to pass my six-month probation. Instead he kept torturing me by delaying it another week. My role at the company was unclear. How can you do your job properly if you know you could be kicked out at any moment?

When a CEO declares he doesn't care about anyone, the business is going to fail.

The CEO also didn't understand why I spent time reading sales books and investing in personal development. He'd never done any.

If you'd ever met the CEO, it's easy to believe he's never done personal development or been on any course that would make him improve or grow. That's how arrogant he was.

Trying to be the saviour, I helped everyone in the office, listened to their concerns, assured them I was on their side and I would do everything I could to protect their jobs. The problem is you can't solve everyone's problems and I didn't pay enough attention to my own clients.

You need to trust your gut instinct and it told me to leave. I should have listened.

The CEO told me magazine costs were so high, they could not afford to keep printing. Normally, you would cut magazine circulation to save costs on printing and postage, however, these magazines were owned by professional trade bodies, which made it complicated, since politics were involved and their members demanded a certain magazine pagination.

So, the CEO told me to rebook customers for 2017. I worked with my team and within three weeks we had rebooked over £65,000 which was amazing. It's always a wonderful feeling when customers invest with you again, it shows you've done something right.

November, 9am, Monday morning, the CEO took me into a room and told me I was to leave the business immediately. I tried to reason with him and he refused to listen. Here's what happened:

- He never said thank you.
- He never even wished me luck, which showed how classless he was, and he avoided eye contact like a coward.
- I was locked out of my iPhone, emails and laptop, so I couldn't call anyone for advice.
- He walked me out of the office like a criminal.

There was no gross misconduct on my part. No written warnings. No violence. No sexism. No homophobia. No criminal behaviour. I never even said a bad thing about the CEO while I was there, verbally or by email – and this was how they treated me?

Imagine being walked out of a business like a criminal. Not getting a chance to say goodbye to your colleagues. Having no access to any emails or even to get the contact details of recruitment consultancies so you can start making calls, it was soul destroying.

I see many managers behave like this and it makes no sense. They believe that being ruthless and cruel will help them stay on top.

It won't. Not long term.

All the best managers care and support others. They can still be tough and make decisions you don't like, however, they do things with integrity.

The CEO behaved like an amateur and karma is beautiful.

You care for people, you have people care for you. You treat people like crap, bad things will happen.

In less than seven months since I was kicked out, the best people left. Most were diplomatic enough to give reasons like a new challenge or working closer to home – when I contacted some of them, they told me the CEO made the office environment unbearable.

Here's the list of people who left. In any big business, this would be a disaster, so imagine how it would affect a small business:

- Editor of the flagship magazine.
- Deputy Editor of the flagship magazine
- Entire sales team of another magazine.
- Entire editorial team of another magazine.
- Freelance editor.
- Business development manager.
- One of the top sales people went to the competition.
- Business Development Manager.
- Our automotive magazine folded since I wasn't there to earn money and the editorial team lost their jobs – the editor was informed two weeks after being diagnosed with cancer.
- They struggled to find a replacement for me and offered the potential candidate a massive drop in salary compared to what I

was earning.

Weeks before Christmas I was unemployed and had no income. I was terrified of the future. Nobody wants to be unemployed before Christmas without any money.

When horrible situations like this happen, you either rise from the ashes or get deeper into a world of self-destruction.

RECAP

- Trust your gut instinct.
- Don't try and solve everyone's problems.
- When the boss says they don't care about anyone, you need to find another job immediately and not hope for the best.

"Success is not final, failure is not fatal. It is the courage to continue that counts." – **Winston Churchill**

"You build on failure. You use it as a stepping stone." – **Johnny Cash**

Chapter Seventeen

When we're desperate, we often make stupid decisions. It takes between 8-16 weeks to find a decent job. With five weeks before Christmas, the thought of not having a job terrified me:

- How would I take care of the family?
- How would I celebrate our wedding anniversary in December?
- How would I buy presents?
- How could I afford to go out with friends?
- How could I afford to do anything?

Shouldn't someone with my experience have seen this coming?

Looking back, I should have thought long-term. When you're firefighting, and dealing with so many internal problems in a business, it's always one day at a time – at the most, I was only looking a week ahead.

You should always be looking 6-12 months ahead. At executive level, it's 3-5 years ahead.

I started applying for jobs although the odds were against me. In December, so many people think about parties, not that much work gets done and everyone is looking forward to a week off watching television repeats, overeating, spending time with family and seeing old friends.

Nobody hires until January and CVs were taking forever to get looked at in December.

Sometimes things happen that you can't explain. Call it karma. Call it fate. Call it luck.

That's what happened when I called a manufacturing publishing business out of the blue. Turns out their popular sales manager Sarah, was going travelling and they wanted a head of sales to manage 8 people. Sarah was great, she started off at the bottom and worked her way up. I respect people that like. The commercial team ranged from a 20-years-old to a 64-years-old, with a mixture of men and women.

The London office was buzzing. The events team were lovely, editorial was friendly and management needed a space filled – I got lucky and secured myself a role as head of sales, although with a £3,000 pay cut.

<u>First warning</u>: when you manage more people, take on more responsibility, have bigger targets, your salary should never get reduced.

The tall, thin stunningly beautiful MD spent most of the interview playing with her hair and reading my CV – yes, completely disorganised and unprepared – and made it clear in front of her team that she would match my previous salary. <u>Second warning:</u> the MD could not be trusted.

What choice did I have? This was the only job I could find. There's nothing worse than doing something you know will lead to disaster. No positive thinking or visualisation will change that.

Contract signed, I had a job before Christmas and into the new year with a family-run business.

Running a team of eight people was non-stop, plus I was expected to sell advertising in the magazine and online, plus sponsorship at conferences and events, many of which had not performed to the high standard they had promised customers.

My predecessor Sarah was loved by everyone and had decided to go travelling the world. Managing staff is very different from selling and her team lacked discipline and focus since nobody was taking care of them.

Here's how I changed the dynamic and sent energy levels through the roof:

- Created power hours every day from 10-11 and 2-3. No email, no updating the CRM system, no meetings, only calling clients.
- Weekly 1-2-1s. This shows staff you care. It's not just about how you are you going to hit your target, it's asking them how are you, how was your weekend and listening to what they say. Show people you care and most of them will deliver a good performance at work.
- Changed the media and information packs which were outdated.
- Weekly call coaching to improve certain staff performances.

- Stopped personal calls during peak times. You can make personal calls over your one hour lunch, during mid-morning or mid-afternoon breaks.

This made huge improvements to team morale and showed them I cared. The same could not be said of MD or CEO.

Third warning: when a new member of staff joins a business, it's vital to make them feel at home. One of those ways is to take them out for a welcome drink or welcome lunch. This is what good companies do. It's what good bosses do. The MD and CEO never took me out for a welcome drink, because they were self-centred and only thought about themselves.

Oprah Winfrey once said that "change doesn't scream at you. It comes in tiny whispers." I should have listened to the whispers and had more emotional intelligence.

This is what happens when daddy runs the business and you have money. The MD forgot about the needs of others and had no compassion or understanding.

Fourth warning: The magazine they printed claimed to be read by 10,000 people, however, there was NO PROOF OF THIS.

Many companies make false claims to earn more money from magazine advertising,

The CEO didn't even know the numbers. Sometimes it was 5,000. Sometimes 10,000. The only numbers that really matter are how many people pay for a magazine and engage with it. He couldn't tell me and continued lying to steal more money from customers.

Luckily, the other members of staff who worked with me in marketing, editorial and events were such a joy to work with, it helped every day.

Larry, the co-owner, was a chain-smoking, hard drinker who did his business in the pub. His clients were mates, he was an excellent schmoozer and brought in a lot of business.

The same couldn't be said about his son - a child of privilege. Private educated and instead of growing a spine and finding work, daddy gave him a job.

Private education ranges from £8,000 – £25,000 a year. That's not including uniform, books, school trips, inflation etc. so Larry's son had about £200,000 worth of education spent on him.

Apart from his posh English accent, you would never think he had any education.

If you spend £200,000 educating a child, laziness is not an option.

Kobe Bryant, one of the top basketball players in the world, gave a wonderful quote: "I can't relate to lazy people. We don't speak the same language. I don't understand you. I don't want to understand you."

Kobe speaks exactly how all ambitious people feel.

As a manager, I had to understand. Why did Larry's son do this? Was it rebellion? No, he seemed to have a great relationship with his father and he was a nice guy to speak to in the pub.

The problem was instead of working he did the following:

1. Talked about football.

2. Took personal calls.

3. Disrupted everyone.

4. Got away with it since nobody wanted to annoy the co-owner in case it affected their job.

Things like this damage a culture and need to be dealt with immediately. I explained to Larry that I had to manage his son like everyone else and that I couldn't show any favours. He agreed.

The other child of privilege was the MD, daughter of the CEO.

She had struggled to get the sales team to do anything and constantly criticised them behind their backs.

The CEO was one of those bosses who thought he knew everything. He took yoga classes although it didn't make him calm or cleanse his soul. His only redeeming feature was that his wife always made everyone feel welcome.

Since he was fixing his other house in Europe, because that was more important than taking care of his staff, I didn't see him much, which was great.

When he started turning up at work, the problems began. We secured a meeting with the manufacturing team at IBM, this was exciting.

IBM are a company everyone wants to do business with. Long history. Big budgets. Experienced personnel.

When you meet a client, big or small, this is what you do:

- Ask questions.
- Show interest.
- Research their website.

Instead the CEO talked nonstop about his business. After 20 minutes he was still yapping, offering slide after slide crammed full of text.

A member of IBM discreetly checked his emails. A few minutes later, another IBM colleague checked his phone. The meeting was a disaster and the CEO kept talking like he was the most important person in the room.

I had to interrupt or we would lose the client, so I mentioned that I read about what IBM were doing in manufacturing since I had spent over an hour researching them. This got a good discussion going.

Afterwards, the CEO asked me how he did. I politely told him that in the future, we should always ask questions first, then present to a client. Also, we shouldn't have 20 PowerPoint slides mainly full of text, we should have no more than 10 slides and make it mainly visual. People remember images much better than text.

Fifth warning: according to research, 21% of corporate professionals are psychopaths. They also suffer from:

- Uncontrolled anger.
- Inability to sustain relationships.

- Violating other people's rights.

- Lack of remorse about other people's distress.

- They specialise in making others uncomfortable – not the good discomfort where you grow, the bad discomfort, where you work in fear.

When I questioned his inability to pitch, the CEO burst into fits of egocentric rage.

"Do you know who I am? I've been a CEO for years, don't you tell me what do to? I was amazing. What the hell do you know, you're only a salesperson?"

I've done hundreds of presentations as well -- undergone a professional and accredited presentation course -- successfully coached sales people from nervous beginners to successful presenters. Rules of presenting to customers:

- Don't talk about yourself first.

- Get the customer engaged.

- Only when you find out what the customers' needs and pain points are, then you present.

- Don't have too many slides. 12 is the maximum.

Getting yelled at by the boss is never an enjoyable experience, especially when they make no sense and act like a spoilt baby.

It's okay to question your boss if it's done respectfully. I said it because I cared and wanted the best for the business. This was done face to face and with the right tone.

LESSON 22 DEALING WITH BAD LUCK

Considering the CEO's arrogant behaviour, I didn't lose my temper. I never yelled or blamed anyone. I kept ploughing on and supporting my team.

I should have stood up to the CEO, however, after my experience standing up to appalling managers at my previous two jobs, it only led to bad consequences.

You get what you tolerate in life. If someone is abusive, and you tolerate it, they will continue to be abusive. Having lost confidence after getting fired, I was terrified about being out of work, so I tolerated the CEO's abuse, and I was convinced things couldn't get worse. Life had other plans.

Ade, senior sales executive, resigned to join the competition. When I asked why, he said he wanted my job and didn't get it.

Ade was a talented sales person with a good heart and was a valuable team player. Being a successful sales person and being a successful manager are different skills. Although he joined the competition, I wished Ade well.

Sixth warning: the CEO and co-owner criticised Ade behind his back, despite having known him for years. I'm not going to repeat their language because it was so offensive. Ade did a good job for us, his event generated £220,000 of sales, yet he did not feel appreciated by the CEO.

You can't fault someone for leaving under those circumstances. Ade behaved with dignity until he left. Judgement day came when trying to find a replacement for Ade.

RECAP

- Listen to the whispers.
- When your boss is a psycho, don't try to change them. Leave the business and work for an employer who respects you.
- You get what you tolerate in life.

"When ill luck begins, it does not come in sprinkles, but in showers."
– Mark Twain

"I believe in luck: how else can you explain the success of those you dislike?" **– Jean Cocteau, French writer, artist, playwright**

Chapter Eighteen

Replacing a member of staff is exhausting. When you work 9-10 hours a day, helping staff, supporting customers, barely replying to all your emails, balancing internal meetings, and God forbid, meetings about meetings, the only time you can look at CVs is on the train home when you should be winding down or over lunch when you should be having a break.

The MD agreed a salary of £33,000 for Adrian's replacement, even though his salary was much more. I spent late nights at home reading CVs, talking to recruitment consultants on the train and sacrificing family time doing interviews after work.

Unfortunately, answers to most first interviews can be found on Google which is why I dislike them. You often don't meet the real person.

Second interviews are where someone shines. You can give them a hypothetical situation and see how they react. You can give them your company brochure and ask them to prepare a presentation. You can bring in different members of staff to see how they connect with them.

Finally, we hired the right person at £33,000. She accepted and I went home to pack for India. We were doing charity work to help children of the leprosy colony, many of whom had spent years suffering from horrendous poverty and begging on the streets. My parents were retired yet they contributed towards the rent of the school every month.

After spending a few days helping others, we planned a family break in Goa.

The MD decided to selfishly email me on my holiday to tell me that she was going to reduce the person's salary and make it up with commission instead.

If you agree a salary, you don't screw someone over. You behave with honour and dignity. These important values cost nothing, yet the MD didn't have them. Cheating another member of staff to save money is not a smart move, yet so many managers do this.

It made me look bad, even though I had done nothing wrong.

People rarely earn commission they are promised, that's how many companies operate. Also, when you start a new job, it often takes 3-4 months to earn money. We were paid quarterly, so it would be a six month wait. Who wants to wait six months to get paid what they're owed?

I replied to the MD informing her what she was doing was wrong. It was vital she treated people with dignity and respect. What she did was wrong. Then my disappointment turned to frustration.

I've been at the company almost 3 months and no member of management had even taken me out for a welcome drink. How do you think I felt? People leave businesses if they're not treated with respect.

Sound fair? I thought so. 30 minutes later, the gutless MD fired me by email saying I was not the right fit for the business. In other words, because I saw through her deceit and lack of integrity, she fired me.

LESSON 23: DON'T EXPRESS EVERY EMOTION

You don't fire someone over a disagreement like this. You fire someone over abuse, theft, racism, sexism, homophobia etc... you don't fire someone because they stand up for staff and ask you to raise yourself to a higher standard.

I'm paraphrasing my reply to the MD since I don't have the email. She didn't have the guts to reply.

I called JS, the bald, bearded affable publisher I had bonded with more than anyone. He wasn't around, so I forwarded the email to ask for advice, since I knew he would care. He didn't.

You always find out who your real friends are when times are tough. JS was a fake.

I didn't sleep all night and the next day at Heathrow Airport, I discreetly emailed the MD so my family wouldn't find out what had happened. It would ruin their holiday. The laptop was switched on.

Yes, I take my laptop on holiday, that's how dedicated I am to whatever company I work for.

When I typed in my password, this is what happened:

- I couldn't access my email.

- I couldn't access internet.

- I had been locked out of the system.

I called the MD's work number and mobile – like a coward, she refused to answer. I called my staff. They were told I had been fired, although had been asked to keep it a secret.

So, I called the CEO – he said the circumstances were regretful.

Regretful? I'm about to get on a plane for eight hours. It's the half-term holiday, which means not many recruitment consultants are around. It costs a fortune to call from India. When looking for work, you don't just ping over a CV, you talk to the recruitment consultants to ask for help. You let them hear your passion and abilities and ask open questions.

They should have waited till I got back from holiday. The CEO said if it was him, he'd want to know as soon as possible. That's the kind of answer a narcissistic jackass would give.

Shweta and I had saved up and planned to donate £600 to Maitree Mission charity to help the street kids. We only gave £300. I couldn't give my £300 since I had no job. I had let these kids down. £300 fed 30 kids for two weeks.

Being unable to help this important charity made me resent the MD and CEO even more. Their grossly unprofessional behaviour had consequences. They say "you can forgive, but you can never forget." I respectfully disagree. I will never forgive or forget the disgraceful and gutless behaviour of the MD and CEO.

<u>RECAP</u>

- Don't write an email in anger.

- You don't have to express every emotion, sometimes it's better you don't.

- Don't tell your boss they're incompetent, even when they are.

"One ought to hold on to one's heart; for if one lets it go, one soon loses control of the head too." – **Friedrich Nietzche**

"A moment of patience in a moment of anger saves you a hundred moments of regret." – **Unknown**

Chapter Nineteen

Warren Buffet recommends 30 minutes a day sitting in peace and quiet. No electronics, no distractions. No music. Just spend time thinking or napping.

This is wonderful advice that I follow every Saturday and Sunday. Often you fall asleep and wake up refreshed. Other times, your eyes widen as a new business idea or better strategy for work comes your way.

Famous nappers include: John F Kennedy. Winston Churchill. Eleanor Roosevelt. Margaret Thatcher. Leonardo Da Vinci – so you're in good company.

Although my previous two jobs turned out to be awful, I'm grateful for the experience.

Without them, I would not have progressed and improved. Without them, I would be thinking short-term. Without them, I would be stuck like so many people are in jobs they absolutely hate.

Things often happen for reasons we can't understand. It's only weeks, or often months later they make sense.

During the holidays, Shweta always spent extra time in India catching up with her family. They're an amazing group of people who will laugh one moment, cry another moment, fight another moment, then be best friends the next day. When Shweta returned to England, I told her the bad news. She was distraught. "How are we going to pay the bills? You should never have reacted like that. How's this going to look when you search for work? Sometimes you just have to do what you're told, even when you disagree with your boss."

As usual, my wife was right. Shweta was seven years younger than me and had never worked in the corporate world, yet she always knew way more than me. I should have written out my frustrations, then pressed delete or taken Mel Robbins' advice and simply counted backwards; 5-4-3-2-1.

At the age of 44, asking your retired parents for a loan to pay the mortgage was humiliating. They kindly helped out while Shweta paid the rest of the bills. As a beauty salon owner, she spent all day listening to people's problems, so had an excellent understanding of office environments, family dynamics and political opinions. She followed up with great advice:

- Take time off.

- Your bosses were terrible. It's not your fault. Find a good boss.

- Choose a job you love, something that gets you out of bed in the morning.

- Just make a difference. Once you make a difference, you will enjoy going to work each day.

- Stop feeling sorry for yourself. It's not an attractive quality in a man.

As usual, my wife was straight to the point. I'm incredibly lucky to have someone as supportive as that in my life. Shweta, like my father, doesn't do hugs. Never said "I love you". Yet, she cared for me more than anyone and was always there when I needed her the most.

LESSON 24: TAKING A BREAK

Being a moody teenager, Shreya dreaded me dropping her at school in case I embarrassed her in front of her friends. I've known her friends since they were 4-years-old, so have no problems high-fiving them and being a dork in their presence. I also wear tracksuit bottoms and rock T-shirts first thing in the morning and have a tendency to sing loudly in the car– thinking about it, I understand why she used to hang her head in shame at the school gate.

After the school run I would go for a 30-minute walk, enjoy the stunning greenery of Milton Keynes, a place unfairly and incorrectly referred to as a concrete jungle. It's family friendly, easy to get around and has one of the lowest unemployment rates in the country.

Instead of wasting my time off work watching DVDs and bad television, I re-read many of the classic books in my library that have helped me grow:

- How to Win Friends and Influence People by Dale Carnegie, which does what it says on the tin. One of the best-selling personal development books of all time and a game changer when it comes to getting on with people.

- The Compound Effect by Darren Hardy. Becoming better each day in small steps.

- The Leader Who Had No Title by Robin Sharma. No matter what your position in life, you can be a leader.

- The 5 Second Rule by Mel Robbins. 8 million people have watched her TED talk for a reason. She's awesome and knows how to transform lives.

- The Charge. Activating the 10 Human Drives That Make You Feel Alive by Brendon Burchard. A master on social media and peak performance brings his magic to the written page.

- Switch by Dan and Chip Heath. Why change is important and how to instigate change in people and companies who don't want to change.

- Losing my Virginity by Richard Branson. Americans are rather amazing when it comes to motivation and positive mental attitude. Branson is still our best export in this sector and inspires in everything he does.

- View From The Top by Aaron Walker. How to lead a life of significance. An inspirational and faith-driven book that opens your mind to new possibilities.

- Change Your Habits, Change Your Life by Tom Corley. After studying and interviewing millionaires, Tom describes what it takes to become successful.

After an hour of deep reading with no distraction from the internet, I took up cooking. Finding time to create simple, delicious fresh recipes, buying ingredients from local grocers, making fabulous dinner every night for my family and friends was therapeutic.

Friday, Saturday and Sunday were spent travelling around the country to see friends I hadn't met in years.

It was a wonderful few weeks. Laughter, hugs, meeting up in parts of the UK I had never been to was so much more refreshing and better for your soul than texts or Facebook. Then I became restless.

This is why if I ever won the lottery, I would never retire. I'd pay off the mortgage, travel and give to charity, but not retire. As humans, we need to be challenged. We need the daily excitement and thrills of doing something that gets us out of bed.

We need progress.

The problem is, most jobs don't get us out of bed. They drain our energy and often leave us feeling helpless.

I called up a few entrepreneurial friends for advice. After 23 years, did I really want to keep working in sales? It had provided me a good life, however, I had recently been burned. Was this a hint? A quiet whisper? Was I meant for something better in life? If so, what?

I went to all the amazing independent coffee shops in Milton Keynes to enjoy a cup of Joe and slice of Victoria sponge cake with friends that had taken up entrepreneurial ventures. Once you have a child, the thought of going back to the daily grind doesn't appeal to most people.

The men I spoke to returned to work and, of course, they missed their kids, but they were glad to get back to their routines.

The women were different. The thought of being away from the child they carried in their stomach for nine months, gave excruciating birth to, and in many cases, breastfed for years, was not an option.

No 9-5 job was worth going back to for that.

Some had tried, come home late at night and not seen their babies all day. On payday, the money they earned went to commuting, food and childcare. Nothing was left over.

What's the point of working hard if you are simply paying for childcare and never see your loved ones?

The entrepreneurs in Milton Keynes made me proud. Sure, you have to work longer hours with your own business, however, you decide those hours, you work around the family.

That's a pretty amazing way of looking at things.

You may not have the salary you once had, but you have something better – freedom to make your own choices.

How do they do it? Well, initially, many had no choice. They didn't have parents who were business people. They decided the life they wanted and built their career around that.

Watching friends give up the corporate grind so they can have a cheese toastie van to feed lunchtime workers and be back for the school run was inspiring. Well done Aida and Bob of Good Times Café.

Observing another friend become of the top bloggers in the country with her website offering advice to writers and novelists. The awesome Lucy V Hay of Bang2Write.

Another friend does the best burgers in town with his incredible flavours and still spends quality time with his wife and bring up the kids together. Congratulations Jonathan Duff of Bandit.

I had no business skills and with my wife being self-employed, the thought of having two entrepreneurs in the family was too risky. Maybe I could have a good life working for somebody else.

Life I want
- Be a good dad and husband.
- Give more value to others.
- Earn enough money to take care of my family.
- Enjoy three holidays a year, two in the UK, one holiday abroad.
- Increase my charity donations from £4,000 to £8,000 a year.
- Have a boss who isn't an idiot.
- Get a dog.

<u>Career I want</u>

- Spend 1 hour a day with family 6 days a week.

- Provide value to others in sales and coaching.

- Avoid small deals. Work on big accounts for big money.

- When I have a holiday, enjoy the holiday and don't spend time working.

- More money I earn, more money I can give to charity.

- Find a boss who shares my values of company culture and family.

- Dog-friendly office.

Finding a job to match my needs proved impossible. After 2 months of searching, applying for hundreds of jobs on LinkedIn, having over 20 interviews in London, every company ticked 1 or 2 boxes, but not all boxes.

If you settle for second best, you end of up somewhere awful... but time was running out. After 2 months of job hunting, we had 5 weeks money left in my account and it takes 4 weeks to earn salary in a new job – that meant I had to find work in a week or else my mortgage would default and our home was in danger of getting repossessed.

I had three job offers on the table and none of them were good enough. Six days left before money ran out.

One of the offers fell through. The boss decided that someone who lost 2 jobs in 3 months was high risk and they had decided to drop the offer. I understand their concern. Would I have done the same? I'd hate to think so. I offered excellent references from people I had worked with. They weren't interested.

Should I accept one of the bad offers? What if they chose somebody else and I have no offers left. I would lose everything.

Five days left before money ran out. I called every recruitment consultant again and many of my LinkedIn contacts. A few of them were kind enough to recommend me to their directors or heads of HR. The roles paid less than what I was earning. Why should I drop my salary for

103

a job I don't want?

Four days left before money ran out. I got a call from Redfish Recruitment, who'd seen my CV on LinkedIn and asked how I felt working for a start-up. Big risk. No security. No guarantee of commission, so I said no.

Redfish was smart. They told me this was a successful South Korean business called G-Smatt that had expanded quickly throughout Asia due to the world-class quality of their product.

Imagine a TV screen on a building. G-Smatt provided the architecture grade LED glass and media content. This was high impact. Stunningly visual. The future of advertising. It was also interactive.

On Chinese New Year, you could download an app and shoot up fireworks on your phone. This would connect to their glass on a building about 50-100m high and you would see fireworks on the building.

An artist working inside a gallery could have their art displayed on the building glass. Imagine your work being displayed 60 – 100 feet high?

A computer gaming company can produce images of their games on the glass and children could interact with it.

Councils who always have problems communicating with their communities could now use the glass to inform drivers of roadblocks, where to park and future renovations.

Buildings could talk to each other and the inhabitants inside. The possibilities were endless.

More importantly this was "disruptive" and that was a massive word in today's fast-changing world.

Apple disrupted the music and mobile industry. Uber disrupted taxis. Airbnb disrupted the hotel business. Amazon disrupted how we buy things – all had become enormous successes.

As part of the start-up, I would hire my own people, build my own culture and work with a boss who had ethics and was a decent human being.

This was a dream come true. Often you join an organisation where everything is set in stone and there's little room for change. Here I was getting a chance to build my vision and create the dream work environment – to avoid all the bad experiences I had before – and create a place where staff would actually want to come to work each day.

Staff should never turn up for a salary which is how most companies operate. When people do work that matters, they go the extra mile for customers, which means more profits for your business and more kudos to you for doing well. Everybody wants to do well in their career.

Three days left before my money ran out.

Had my interview over the phone with Dr Orhan Ertughrul, a Cambridge-educated highly intelligent and thoughtful CEO. Spent an entire day researching G-Smatt Global, shared my thoughts on my experience working with customers around the world, asked lots of open questions which showed I was interested and connected with my new boss.

I had other offers on the table and needed an answer quickly. He told me straight away he wanted someone like me to work for his business and invited me to create a presentation on what I would achieve in my first 90 days.

Two days left before my money ran out.

I put together the mother of all presentations. Spent hours prepping it, longer rehearsing it, kept it to only 9 slides. Made it highly visual. Video recorded myself to check body posture, arm waving, eye contact, confidence and tone of voice. Watched several TED talks to improve even more. Showed how we would do business as a start-up. The number of calls we could make per day. The number of meetings per week.

The next thing I knew it was 1am. That's how much I wanted this job. I got into the flow and had lost track of time.

Have you ever had a wonderful feeling about a business that was right for you? This was it...

One day left before money ran out

I decided to take a risk and provide another presentation on the culture we needed to create in the office:

- An environment staff want to work in.

- Give them something bigger than themselves to work towards.

- Offer free coffee – not the cheap machine crap with cardboard cups and unnatural milk, but quality Nespresso or Cafetiere with fresh ground coffee.

- Take them out for weekly lunch as a thank you.

- Individual meetings every Monday to talk about goals and dreams of the staff.

Zero days left to find a job and I had £37 left in my bank account, which paid for petrol to and from Oxford and the extortionate parking prices in the city centre.

Malmaison was a stunning five-star hotel in Oxford which was previously a prison for centuries. The rooms are converted cells. It's popular with tourists and was renowned for excellent service and scrumptious food. This was where the interview took place. How ironic. A job interview in a former prison.

Orhan appreciated my effort and even added he would offer free medical, generous company pension and a heavily discounted gym membership. With 30 years of business experience, he also believed deeply in taking care of staff and giving them the best environment to work in.

He had one concern. I had lost two jobs in three months!

Here it is again. The bad experiences in my previous roles had come back to haunt me. This was my last chance, there was no way I could return to mediocrity of an average career.

I recapped on my sales success, my charity work, that I was a better person because of the pain I had endured.

He held up his hand. Didn't want to hear any excuses. I was devastated. Nothing less than heart and soul had gone into this job interview. I wanted it so badly. An awkward pause followed.

"We all make mistakes," said Orhan. "We all suffer bad luck. Your track record speaks for itself. You've not just delivered an excellent presentation but you want to run my business like I do. I still have other candidates to interview. We will be in touch."

There was still hope.

Sometimes, all you need is hope.

Waiting for an answer from a job interview causes butterflies to have a riot in your stomach. This had bigger impact, since I had nothing left, no emergency savings, no bonds to cash, no ISA waiting to mature, nothing.

I stared at the mobile like it would magically ring. Kept refreshing my email. Checked spam. Stared outside in case the postman delivered a job offer by special delivery. I went over the interview again and how it related to my life goals.

- Spend 1 hour a day and all-day Sunday with family – Yes, Orhan didn't believe in working all the time. He was a family man. Hard work, yes. Insanely hard work every day and night, no.

- Help others first – Yes. Orhan was a Christian and believed in helping others first.

- Don't do lots of small deals, work on big accounts for big money – Yes. G-Smatt deals started at £30,000 for exhibitions and £500,000 - £4,000,000 for buildings.

- When I get holiday, I actual take a holiday and don't spend time working – Yes, Orhan didn't believe in working on holidays or weekends.

- More money I earn, more money I can give – Yes - my salary went up 20% as I was now a director of sales which meant my charity donations increased.

- Find a boss who shares my values of company culture and family – Yes, amazing.

- Dog-friendly office. If we hit target in Year 2, we would get a dog that everyone would love and adore.

If I didn't get this job, we would lose our home. The phone rang. I took a deep breath and answered. It was my mother asking if I heard anything. I quickly hung up.

Five minutes later, it rang again. It was Redfish Recruitment. They were pushing for an answer and couldn't get hold of Orhan who was on voice mail.

Minutes turned into hours. My heartbeat became a painfully loud thud. I visualised the job. Visualised the success. Saw my name signed on the dotted line.

The mobile rang. It was Stef at Redfish. "After careful consideration..."

No good conversation ever starts "after careful consideration." What was I going to do now?

A long pause followed: "G-Smatt Europe would like to offer you the job."

Euphoria. Elation. Excitement.

At the last minute, G-Smatt Europe had saved my life. I had been given another chance and I was not going to waste it.

<u>RECAP</u>

- Rest 30 minutes a day in peace and quiet.
- If things don't go according to plan, it's okay to take time off and regroup.
- Decide the life you want and build a career around that.
- Don't settle for second best. Go for what you want.

"Mornings belong to whatever is new. Afternoon is for napping and letters." – **Stephen King**

"Two things are infinite: the universe and naps; and I'm not sure about the universe." – **Albert Einstein**

Chapter Twenty

I was the first full-time employee hired by G-Smatt Europe, innovative producers of architecture grade LED glass and interactive media content. 80% of new buildings are made of glass, so there was a strong market out there.

People are surprised when I tell them I work in architecture and construction with no qualifications, especially with my work history too: The Guardian was public sector and digital media, Marketing Week was marketing, promotions, and incentives, Informa was shipping, ports, transport and logistics and the last few roles were in engineering, then manufacturing. But I never had experience in any of these sectors.

So, I immersed myself into these varied areas and learned quickly, however, it's the great questions you ask, the insight you share, the solutions you provide to a customer and the authentic service you give that makes you valuable.

This was the same in each industry.

Sure, you have to make some tweaks here and there. For example, when selling to lawyers, they don't care about visuals, they want written facts. In shipping, it's about shaking someone's hand and doing business over a drink, preferably the alcoholic kind. Events are all face to face. IT, it's over email. In architecture, it's about touching the feet of architects and reminding them of their God-like status. They rarely take phone calls or reply to emails.

When I got the role of director of sales at G-Smatt Europe, I was told they expected me to take care of the marketing as well – it's an increasingly common thing for companies to give staff extra responsibility without paying them extra.

I had 'director' in my title. That wasn't just something I could do a few hours a week, I had to find time for marketing and I didn't have any more hours in the day than anybody else.

My initial reaction was like most people. If I work an extra 10 hours a week and deal with extra pressure, shouldn't I get paid more...?

I already had a generous payrise to become director of sales, my first time ever moving into this senior position. I had also become part of the leadership team, so I had an influence over important company decisions from staff hires to strategy.

While reading my valuable SUCCESS magazine, I was reminded of a wonderful quote by the late, great Jim Rohn, considered by many to be the father of personal development.

LESSON 25: ALWAYS DO MORE THAN WHAT YOU GET PAID FOR.

- It's how you move onto bigger and better things.
- It creates enormous goodwill for the company you work for.
- If you have a decent boss, they will appreciate it.
- You pick up so many extra skills along the way which will be useful long term.
- Nobody ever died doing an extra 30-60 minutes a day in the office.

Orhan was smart enough to understand the importance of investing in people. Many companies claim their staff are their most important asset, however, when you talk to the staff, you get a different perspective.

Luckily, we hired a fabulous marketing agency called H20 Creative to work with me which made life easier. They had an eclectic group of people from the lovable, brilliant Italian Vincenza to the down-to-earth and reliable Iain – they created designs, fonts, logo, colours, posters, brochures and a marketing direction, while I worked on implementation with Orhan.

In 23 years of business, I've discovered that most staff are not appreciated. Most staff are not paid what they deserve. So many people in small, medium and big corporations, are not treated with enough care or respect or have bosses that look out for them. When staff are treated well, they perform better and the company benefits.

Sure, there's always going to be a few people who take advantage but overall, it had advantages. It's how great companies are born. It's how companies stay around for decades.

I attended marketing seminars at the Festival of Marketing and learned from masters like Simon Coulson and Dan Kennedy. I digested book after book on marketing and leadership. Sacrificed regular weekends to attend courses in leadership and personal development – all paid for by G-Smatt Europe. They invested heavily in me and got it returned tenfold by my performance.

Cramming everything into a day is hard, especially when you have two roles, so I cut back on personal social media, only watched TV at weekends and focused relentlessly. Here's how a typical productive day looks:

- 8am – 9am. Learn.
- 9am – 10am. Answer emails.
- 10am – 10.30am. Team meeting.
- 10.30am – 11.30am. Social media – for PR, marketing and branding.
- 11.30am - 12.30. Prospecting for new clients.
- 12.30pm - 1.30pm. Lunch – turn the mobile off, lock computer screen, get some fresh air and at least once a week have lunch with a friend.
- 1.30pm - 2.30pm. Reply to emails.
- 2.30pm - 3.30pm. Whatever the boss needs doing.
- 3.30pm - 4.30pm. Marketing by post. Checking on campaigns. Making tweaks.
- 4.30pm - 5.30pm. Cold calling.
- 5.30pm - 6.00. Review my day and prepare tomorrow.

A couple of evenings a week attend networking events for a few hours; 50 hours at work, plus 4 hours networking. Once a week that routine is broken when I spend a day out of the office seeing new clients and servicing customers.

Marketing campaigns need to be implemented across a range of platforms. Although digital has the fastest growth - and it works well - digital is not enough.

Clients are bombarded with emails and simply can't reply to them all. Magazine advertising doesn't have the impact it once had, however, is still important for branding. Shaking hands at networking events is key in most industries. Sending valuable material in the post to a customer is gold dust since hardly anyone does it. It can be a magazine, research, a newspaper article, as long as it has insight and teaches the customer something new.

Being positive attracts positive people. We hired some of the most enthusiastic and positive people I have ever worked with at G-Smatt Europe which makes the long journey to work everyday an absolute joy.

RECAP

- Do more than what you get paid for.
- Learn new skills every day.

"Power means happiness. Happiness means hard work and sacrifice." **– Beyoncé**

"Nothing can substitute for hard work." **– Andrew Agassi, former world tennis champion**

Chapter Twenty-One

I've attended over 500 evening events where companies gave talks, launched new products and tried to sell themselves. Majority of these events are pretty similar; most guests don't know each other and nobody introduces them, so they don't talk to each other.

Often, there's no name badges, so nobody knows who is who. A director speaks for 10-15 minutes and isn't that exciting. His subordinates applaud. Another director talks about himself and is equally uninteresting. A joke is made between the directors that they find funny and nobody else finds funny. They serve alcohol with crisps and nuts like it's a cheap bar.

If they do serve hor d'oeuvres, there's never enough and guests swarm around like zombies at feeding time.

Nobody collects business cards, so you can't keep in touch with guests. When you do keep in touch it's with a mass marketing clichéd email, which has no personal value.

Goody bags contain memory sticks with the directors' presentations which nobody will ever watch. The company brochure is often thrown in where they talk about what makes them unique is "customer service" the most overrated and underpromised phrase in business – if a business has nothing useful to offer, they often default to good customer service.

The G-Smatt launch party was still talked about by business people in Oxford, six months after it took place.

Why did it work?

Because when you've been to so many awful parties, you know how to create a fabulous one. You produce a legendary event, people want to do business with you. Even better, they tell their business colleagues at other networking events about you which is free publicity.

As a result, we had businesses calling us and emailing us. In one case, a local MP even told people about how good our launch party was and that we were a company to look out for.

If you spent £50,000 on an advertising campaign, you couldn't get this kind of publicity. So, here's what we did:

LESSON 26: HOW TO CREATE A SUCCESSFUL PARTY.

- Offer an abundance of delicious fresh food from a local supplier.

- Make it all about the guests.

- Have future technology. We're all fascinated by the future and installed Virtual Reality stations for everyone to "walk around South Korea" or "swim in Hawaii and hear the sound of the waves."

- The welcome speech by Orhan was only five minutes. He talked about vision and told a great story.

- Five minutes from a special guest – after months of persistence, I secured the Lord Mayor of Oxford, Jean Fooks. She was a joy to speak to and guaranteed people would attend.

- Five minutes from our global CEO, Ho Joon Lee, which had his usual charm and boldness.

- All guests received a memorable goody bag – not a memory stick with your company info. Never a brochure. Something they enjoyed - a good quality bottle of red wine.

- Have an amazing team. The dedication, hard work and care shown by my colleagues at G-Smatt Europe was moving. We all believed in our culture and had the same common goal – wow the customer.

- Give to charity. We donated £1 for every business card we received from a guest and then topped it up giving £350 to Sobell House Hospice and £300 to Oxford Children's Hospital.

- The only thing we would have changed was having friends volunteer. Most new events from unknown businesses have 50-60% turnout. We had 81% and people were queuing at the door.

RECAP

- Stop talking about your product.
- Make people feel special.
- Have a guest speaker who will attract more guests.

"At a dinner party, one should eat wisely but not too well, and talk well but not too wisely," – **W. Somerset Maugham, playwright and author**

"Chase the vision, not the money. The money will end up following you," – **Tony Hsieh, CEO, Zappos**

Chapter Twenty-Two

Sales and selling has changed dramatically in the last few years:

a) Everyone is busier than ever.

b) Cold calling rarely works like it used to.

c) More people sell by email rather than pick up the phone.

d) Decision makers rarely answer all their emails, so most sales emails get ignored.

e) Companies do about 80% of the research on you and your business on the internet before they make contact. That means they also do 80% research on your competitors.

Selling may have changed, but one thing hasn't. I attended a recent conference where Ruth Badger, runner-up in the second series of The Apprentice TV series, summed it up perfectly: "people buy people" she bellowed in her lovely Wolverhampton accent.

"You can have the best software, the fanciest phone, the nicest clothes, but unless you are a trusted and world class product such as Amazon, Facebook, Google or Apple, people will always buy people."

Distraction is one of the biggest challenges facing everyone. Here's what disrupts us in our normal working day:

a) Sales people calling.

b) Internal issues.

c) Text messages.

d) Facebook messages.

e) Phone ringing.

f) Work mobile ringing.

g) Personal mobile ringing.

h) Answering a colleague's phone when they're away from their desk.

i) Boss needs a few minutes of your time, which always takes longer.

j) A colleague needs a few minutes of your time, which always takes longer.

k) Visitors – postman, salesman, someone lost, DHL, Fedex, incorrect post.

l) Emails from friends about going out.

m) Office gossip about celebrities, government and news.

n) Work email.

o) Spam.

p) Work emails you wish were spam.

q) Meetings about meetings.

r) Friends sending Youtube videos.

s) Friends sending jokes.

t) Discussing what you're doing over the following weekend when it's only Monday.

Research shows in an eight-hour day, most people don't get more than 3-4 hours work done due to constant distractions. When you try and sell your product – which we all have to do – it's getting harder to get people's attention.

I don't believe cold calling is dead. Anyone who claims it is can't sell or they are trying to peddle their software. It's still important to spend one hour a day calling cold clients, since that will always lead to 10% annual revenue and that 10% can become 20-30% the following year depending on how excellent your customer service is and how valuable your product is.

The best times to cold call are between 4-6pm. Why? Because most people don't bother calling after 4pm and that's when I get hold of most clients.

Sending emails or LinkedIn inmails, if done properly, is beneficial. Most people don't know how to write emails. How many emails remain in your inbox for months or get immediately deleted? That's how difficult it is.

I've worked out a formula which has helped me generate more interest from customers and will help you get more value from your customers:

Dear xxxx (never send an email without the person's name, it shows a real lack of class. Nobody should ever read an email addressed simply "hi there" "hiya" or "hi").

I am writing to you because... (people need to know why you are contacting them and the reason has to benefit them, it's not about you).

Then you can say one paragraph about your business and why your business will benefit them.

If you have nothing to send in the post, explain you will be in the area meeting a client. Give the name of the client to make it real. Then ask for 10 minutes for a coffee.

PS (this is something you know that shows you have researched the client or the business. If the person is junior or middle management, make it about them. If it's an executive or CEO, make it about the business. It can be something you read on their LinkedIn profile or website).

Don't include attachments! 60% of emails are now read on mobiles, so emails need to kept short and sweet. No sensible person opens attachments from someone they don't know.

Promise it won't take longer than 10-15 minutes and even if they don't use your product, they will still walk away with more knowledge. Here's an example:

Dear Sebastian,

I am writing to you because I read your article on LinkedIn about you wanting to find innovative ways of marketing your business next year.

Since we provide innovative media facades that are used by high profile clients in Shanghai, South Korea, Tokyo and England for high impact disruptive marketing, it makes sense to see how we can help you.

I will be near your office next Wednesday meeting Samsung about their upcoming technology exhibition and would like to meet for coffee for 10-15 minutes. I respect that you're incredibly busy and even if you don't use our product, you will still walk away with more knowledge.

PS I noticed on your LinkedIn profile you have volunteered for Prince's Trust, well done. I was volunteer chairman of Informa's Prince's Trust fundraising effort in 2014 which we won the Corporate Social Responsibility Award.

Kind regards

Niraj Kapur

Mobile

email

https://uk.linkedin.com/in/nkapur

LESSON 27: SALES HAS CHANGED MORE IN FIVE YEARS THAN THE LAST 25 YEARS.

Nobody will buy on a first call. They will have coffee, read your material, meet you again with their colleagues. Maybe talk to you some more on email and phone. Meet you again. This sales dance is not because they can't make a decision, it's to ensure you don't mess them about like so many people have done in the past.

Between 5 – 8 people are involved in the decision-making process, so always ensure you have more than one contact at any company. Always know who are the influencers and get them on your side.

Networking, trade shows, events and exhibitions, apart from referrals, are still the best way to do business because you are shaking hands, seeing smiles, body language and hearing tone. There's no technology to distract you and it's the fastest way to build rapport.

At an exhibition, you get 2-3 minutes at someone's stand. After that, offer to follow-up since they're at an exhibition to do business, not listen to you. Show massive interest in their product. Ask open questions such as what is so unique about your product, why launch it now, how is it better than what your competition is doing?

As a bonus, offer to introduce them to an editor/journalist/blogger or someone who can promote their business for free. This creates tremendous goodwill.

Conferences and exhibitions have networking events. If they don't, they should have. So many people check their phone to avoid networking or sit alone to steer clear of the crowd. The most fascinating people are often by themselves.

When I first signed BT as a sponsor for £25,000, I met the decision-maker at an event, having lunch by himself. He was too full of British reserve to approach anyone. I had no idea who he was and I thought he'd like some company for 20 minutes.

After all, who likes eating alone?

I asked lots of questions and got him talking about his business. Only in the last five minutes did I tell him how The Guardian could benefit.

Four months and two meetings later, we had a signed contract, simply because I made the effort to say hello.

There are more people than ever offering you the latest sales software to help you hit target. They're also warning companies that sales people will become obsolete.

All the top sales people I worked with five years ago are still successful. Five years from now, they will still be successful because they follow the 27 Lessons outlined in this book.

If you can sell, you can enjoy more success and have a greater opportunity to have the career that you want.

RECAP

- Learn how to write great emails
- Emails need to be read on a Smartphone.
- Try to meet customers face to face.
- Introduce customers to people who can help them.
- Great technology will never replace someone who can sell properly.

"I have never worked a day in my life without selling. If I believe in something, I sell it, and I sell it hard." – **Estée Lauder**

"There are no rules in selling and you have to know them all." – **Anthony Iannarino**

INTERVIEWS: PEOPLE WHO SELL EVERY DAY BUT AREN'T IN SALES

Learning from successful people is one of the best ways to grow and progress your career. Even if you want to stay in the same job, learning from others will always help you do better.

The following people, from SMEs (small and medium-sized enterprises), to entrepreneurs, to CEOs of top corporate companies, have kindly shared advice, insight and knowledge in how they use sales every day, even though they're not sales people....

Gemma Burnikell, MD, GEM MEDIA Marketing Consultancy

GEM MEDIA helps SMEs get the brand awareness and sales they deserve through comprehensive Marketing communications such as Social Media, Web Design, Email, Graphic Design, Events and PR.

The Founder of GEM MEDIA, Gemma Burnikell promoted local events, worked in B2B Marketing, reached Marketing Manager level, managing employees, budgets and trying new mediums, when she decided she wanted more and naturally the next step was Director level. Now, Gemma works with businesses in all sectors.

How important is sales in your company?

Sales is a fundamental part of the business. It is good to be busy working on projects, however to support growth we need revenue, GEM MEDIA dedicates a couple of hours each day to scope out new business and arrange meetings where possible. Even if they do not become a sale, it is a new contact added to the network which is vital for relationship building.

What skills do people need when selling?

People need to approach sales in a humanised, friendly and personal way. Stay clear of extremely formal approaches or a lengthy impersonal email which will make the reader switch off. Keep it short, sweet and to the point.

What's the best sale you've ever done and how did it happen?

I needed to print a document, Googled 'Internet Café in Milton Keynes' and up came 'XpressoNet' in Xscape MK. The website design and layout was not user-friendly, so I sent them an e-mail explaining what I do and how I can help their business. They invited me in for a meeting. I developed an excellent relationship with the owner and supported them with Marketing strategy, point of sale and PR.

What advice do you have for anyone selling?

1. Be yourself. Too many people try and hide their personality or values and I think these are elements we should not hide. It is good to be human and not a 'sales robot' as people buy off people.

2. Be persistent. Everyone lives hectic lifestyles, that your email or call back could be forgotten about. Remind them that you are still here and connect with them on Social media in the interim, so they can see all the great work you are doing.

3. Show you care. Outside of work people have a lot of personal matters. Don't come across like all you want to do is make the sale. Show you care about them.

www.gemmediamk.com

Mike Rea, CEO, Idea Pharma

Mike Rea has worked in global pharma strategy for over 25 years. Regarded as an industry thought leader in innovation, Mike has helped lead the strategic direction of over 100 pharmaceutical brands, including the top 2 launches of 2015, and over half of the 50 fastest growing drugs in the 2010-15 window.

Mike has been named as one of the 100 Most Inspiring People in Healthcare in 2011, 2013 and 2015 (PharmaVoice) and voted one of the Top 10 Innovators in Pharma (PharmaPhorum).

Outside work, Mike owns an independent record label (Medical Records), organises the street food/food truck festival **MXMK**, and cycles really slowly.

How important is sales in your company?

The most important thing we do. Sales is how we get work. When it gets called sales, people have a different relationship. It's selling, but consultative. It depends on the customer needs. All sales should be bespoke rather than one size fits all. A bit like architecture, you have to adapt, adjust and wow a client.

What skills do people need when selling?

As the CEO, I am always selling. Different members of the team sell as well in addition to supporting the client. I travel a lot, especially across USA since selling is based on trust and you build trust face to face more than over the phone or email. It's hard being away from family, however, that's the sacrifice you make for success.

What's the best sale you've ever done and how did it happen?

There was a project we worked on for a year which was a game changer in our industry. We had to sell it to several people from influencers to decision-makers which meant several meetings. There was tremendous excitement every time we pitched. We do simple pitches. Some are even sketched on paper which is unique since everyone uses slides.

Being British in the USA helps enormously. Our humour and sincerity goes down well. You have to give people what they want not what they need, because sometimes clients don't know what their need is – or it can change during a conversation.

What advice do you have for anyone selling?

Get comfortable with the idea that sales is vital – and a lot of it is about you and how you connect with people. Build intrinsic value. Be authentic. Sales is about trust. It's always about the customers. At the same time, you have to give value. I also read a lot of books about my industry and other industries since I find it useful to learn from other industries. When Steve Jobs was trying to find a way to get the mouse to move for the iMac, he couldn't find a solution in the technology industry, he found it in the health industry, using the roller from deodorants.

http://ideapharma.com/

Mark Sanderson, screenwriter

Mark creates film and television projects for producers and studios, but also offers consultation services for film projects during the development and production stages.

The Los Angeles-based screenwriter, author, and script consultant has written thirty-four screenplays in many genres during twenty years of working in Hollywood.

His eleven produced films have premiered on television and at film festivals, and have been distributed globally. He's also been blessed to work with Academy Award winning producers, veteran film directors, and he's written films starring Academy Award, Emmy, and Golden Globe acting nominees.

How important is sales in your company?

It's extremely important because I'm not only selling myself as a screenwriter and maintaining my professional reputation, but also selling my ideas in the form of pitches and completed screenplays. As a screenwriter, you're always selling, and that's why you have to know your abilities, your goals, and what types of films your producers are looking to make.

What skills do people need when selling?

Conveying an idea to the client. This is why you have to know your product intimately. I'm usually pitching stories to producers, and I have to make sure they clearly understand the concept I'm trying to sell. When I'm trying to sell my completed projects, I'm trying to match the right screenplay with the right producer for the best chance at a sale. Another important skill is to be personable and open to new ideas from my clients about my projects. They are looking for someone who is a team player and collaborator.

What's the best sale you've ever done and how did it happen?

My first sale of an original screenplay. It was a long, seven-year journey from the time I completed writing the project, to the time it went into production. It's extremely difficult to sell an original screenplay in Hollywood, and I was lucky to beat the odds. The producers were looking to make this genre of film and had just started their new production company. It was an example of being at the right place and the right time, and we know that in sales, timing can be vital to selling your product.

What advice do you have for anyone selling?

Do not be discouraged if you don't immediately sell your product during your first attempt into the marketplace. A sale can take years to find a buyer. It's also important that you know your product intimately before you venture out and try to sell it. You can also up your odds for a sale by targeting those potential buyers who actually are interested in what you're selling. I don't waste time trying to sell a big action movie to a small company that only makes heartfelt dramas. Know your audience, do your homework, be prepared, go forward and flourish.

www.fiveoclockblue.net

Shweta Kapur, Salon Owner, Director and Head Therapist at Harmony Beauty Therapy

The eldest of five siblings, Shweta grew up in a single parent family in Delhi, India. Sales training started from a very young age when she had to convince her mother, who had a limited income, for a daily subscription to the English language newspaper, The Times of India, because she was the only one who read it after her dad passed away.

She worked in her parents' business after school and weekends. Moved from India to the UK at the age of 18 after an arranged marriage. Gained her beauty qualification from London College of Beauty Therapy and Milton Keynes College where she won Student of the Year.

After running another salon for minimum wage, she decided to start her own business to offer superior treatments and take much better care of customers.

In 2004 Harmony Beauty Therapy was born. It was a tough start for the 24-year-old, with no friends or family close by and a baby to look after. 14 years later Harmony is the most successful salon in Buckingham, England.

What your company do?

Harmony Beauty Therapy offers a wide range of health and beauty treatments, specialising in results-driven anti-aging treatments.

How important is sales in your company?

Sales is an integral part of our business policy. We are selling a lifestyle and a philosophy of wellness with our treatments and products.

What skills do people need when selling?

Listening to your target audience and understanding what they are looking for – then through your product knowledge, you can sell the right products to them.

Training is also very important. I attend courses every year and read beauty magazines to stay on top of my skills and learn about my industry. Empowering staff is equally important. I used to do all the work and there's only so far you can go by yourself. I enjoy work more by hiring staff and coaching them on how customers should be treated and how treatments need to be performed. It's also important to over deliver on what you promise.

What's the best sale you've ever done and how did it happen?

The best sale happened 14 years ago when I booked my first client, Jane. I would spend 12 hours a day front of house at a gym offering treatments. It was soul destroying since nobody knew me, so why would they spend money? When I got my first client, I treated her like royalty. She was so happy, she recommended her daughter, then granddaughter, then several of her friends. Today she's still my best client and luckily, she has also become a close friend.

What advice do you have for anyone selling?

Be a good listener. Understand what is going on in your industry. You must never stop learning. Knowing why you want to do something is more important that just doing it.

www.harmonybeautytherapy.co.uk

James Epstein
Subscriptions Manager at Lloyd's List

After graduating from law school during the height of the recession, James struggled to find a law-related job. Not wanting to sit around and do nothing he searched for a job in sales/marketing.

His first opportunity arose as a telesales executive selling delegate spaces to insurance summits in London and Bermuda.

With no previous sales experience, he was taken on as a temp for a month. After achieving 200% against target, he was promoted to selling the insurance publication that the summit stemmed from.

The next big change came from within, as the company underwent a massive restructure. The sales teams were reorganised and he found himself managing a new account management team. He now manages reps working as far away as Australia and Singapore.

What does your company do?

Lloyd's List is a specialist provider of maritime news, information and insight. With its routes dating back to 1734, it is one of the oldest publications in the market and means it is the most trusted enabling our readers to rely on the information we provide.

How important is sales in your company?

Vital. We pride ourselves on having the best quality publications and information in the market. However, with the markets the way they have been, they do not sell themselves. We have a large team consisting of account managers and business development reps. They will try and penetrate markets that may not have otherwise have heard of us.

What skills do people need when selling?

I always say there are three types of knowledge that you need to have.

- Sales knowledge.
- Industry knowledge.
- Product knowledge.

There are loads of other attributes that they need to have. Tenacity and determination are top among them. Sales is hard and without those qualities, it's easy to give up.

What's the best sale you've ever done and how did it happen?

I upsold a single user license for the insurance publication to a worldwide license. It took a lot of hard work. Utilising the existing relationship, I had to find referrals in different offices. Then calling round different offices and speaking to several people, setting them up with some trial access and then collating feedback. Then finding and approaching the right people to show how this service could benefit different staff members in different roles.

What advice do you have for anyone selling?

Remember that there is no secret recipe to ensuring that every call results in a sale. Every sales skill you learn, every action you take only increases the probability that someone will buy from you. Some days can be really hard, but if you do the right things and are hardworking, it will pay off.

www.lloydslist.com

Neville Raschid, Film Producer

Selling my first movie in 2006 was tough since I had done two impossible things. A British movie that wasn't a period piece and a comedy with no stars called Flirting with Flamenco. So, I looked into the Bollywood movies since I had grown up watching them. They want recognisable names and I had no connections, so I made the first British Bollywood movie with a British cast and crew.

I have since produced a succession of profitable micro-budget British movies like Ealing Comedy, Naachle London, UnHallowed Ground and the upcoming horror White Chamber.

How important is sales in your company?

I'm selling every hour of every day. Selling to my wife to let me quit my successful job as an accountant to go into the unstable world of making a movie. Selling to financers to invest in my movies. Selling to the cast and crew that this movie would work on a tiny budget.

What skills do people need when selling?

Find out a person's needs. Too many people think about their own needs, that's not selling. What does the other person want?

You need to build good teams, you can't do it all by yourself.

When you love what you do, you have to keep going.

What's the best advice you could give someone?

What does your buyer need? Ask questions. Research. Most people don't do this and it's vital. The bigger the project, the more questions you have to ask.

www.aviaryfilms.com

Mike Mack, Business Facilitator, Coach and Speaker

Mike is the author of *Remarkable Service – How to Keep Your Doors Open*, a sought-after consultant, coach, trainer and speaker, holds an MBA from Athabasca University and is a proud member of Synergy Network (Edmonton).

He has been helping business teams maximise their potential since 2006 with the use of tailored consulting and training programs, along with coaching advice. For Mike, it's about "trusted collaboration" with his customers.

He is passionate about helping companies increase their customer satisfaction, employee retention and achieve profitable growth. He supports business in the areas of: Customer Service, Sales Growth, Team Building, Leadership Development and Strategic Planning, with the objective of making the overall customer experience remarkable.

How important is sales in your company?

It is a vital component to any business. You must continually drop pebbles and chase the ripples of opportunity.

I focus on structured time each week for business development and relationship building. Follow-up is also key as you can never leave anything to chance when it comes to sales.

What skills do people need when selling?

Exceptional interpersonal skills, relationship building savvy, with the ability to communicate effectively with your customer and prospective customer. You must always listen more than you talk when meeting with a customer.

In addition, discipline and focus are critical. You need to know your target customer and discover who the decision maker is.

What's the best sale you've ever done and how did it happen?

There are several examples I can think of but one that comes to mind occurred in the spring of 2012. (This customer still does business with me today). I was referred to this company and met 4 senior managers of the organisation. That meeting was all about listening to their needs and better understanding how I could best support them. When returning a week later to present my proposal the President was in attendance for this meeting and I would be meeting him for the first time. I now had to connect and interact with 5 people in the boardroom. After some open and interactive dialogue, the CFO said to me, "you really captured what we need and I am impressed that you listened so well during our first meeting." He said that they will discuss my proposal and get back to me in a few days. The President chimed in and asked if I could leave the boardroom for a few minutes. I patiently waited and they invited me back in the boardroom with a smile and a handshake, stated that they would like me to start working with them the following week.

What advice do you have for anyone selling?

Be focused, be patient and constantly demonstrate value before ever expecting a cheque from a new customer. Connect with them and make the conversation all about them and less about your products and services.

www.mikemack.ca

Safia Ali, Mum, Wife, Caterer at Saf's Kitchen

Originally from Glasgow, Safia worked in sales/retail for many years and moved to Milton Keynes after getting married. She continued to work in retail and now has two beautiful girls while still running her own business – Saf's Kitchen – which produces traditional Indian cuisine using locally produced ingredients.

How important is sales in your company?

Hugely important. It pays for the running of our life.

What skills do people need when selling?

Confidence with lots of personality. I spent hours poring over recipes which gives me the confidence to promote my business to the community.

As proud as I am of our delicious food, we spend a lot of time talking to our customers. Our takeaway food, cooking lessons and event catering are so much more than transactions. People are giving up their time and money, so you need to be grateful, spend time talking to them and make them feel welcome. I guess part of that is my Scottish upbringing where I love to chat.

What advice do you have for anyone selling?

Have a great support network. My mother helps when cooking for big events, while my husband, Ish, runs around, does all the transportation and setting up. My daughters are always there to keep energy levels high and my friend, Jess, supports us and works her socks off. It's important to enjoy what you do and create a team dynamic.

https://en-gb.facebook.com/SafsKitchen.mk/

Richard Rosser, CEO, B4 Business

Born in Oxford, Richard attended Dragon School and Abingdon School, both in Oxford, before graduating from Southampton University and joining, (what is now), PricewaterhouseCoopers.

He returned to Oxford in 1992 to help his father in a new publishing venture selling advertising for golf club location maps.

They moved into other sports including football, cricket, rugby league and union before making a change of direction, deciding to turn their attention to Oxford with the launch of *In Oxford Magazine* in 2002 and *B4 Magazine* in 2006.

But having developed beyond a magazine into a networking organization, *B4* now has a community of over 600 members who network through the magazine, website and regular high-quality networking events and dinners.

B4 also organizes the annual Business in Oxford event, established in 2013 to help showcase and connect Oxfordshire businesses during a day of presentations, exhibitions and networking.

How important is sales in your company?

Vital, it's the lifeblood of any company, with the exception of those with unlimited resources or other forms of funding. However you dress it up, no sales = no money = no business.

What skills do people need when selling?

Relationship building is key to gain the confidence of your customers.

Patience – nobody likes a desperate salesperson.

Confidence – in your product that what you are selling is of value to your customer.

Care – if you don't care about your customers then why should they care about you or your product?

Awareness – when to turn the relationship from 100% professional to 99% professional and 1% friendly and take it from there.... nobody likes to be called 'mate' in the first call!

What's the best sale you've ever done and how did it happen?

Two very different sales:

Publishing:

We were introduced to the developer of Oxford Castle when they took over the site before the opening in 2006. We negotiated a three-year deal with the tenants worth £150,000 over three years for exposure in *In Oxford Magazine*.

Agency:

I negotiated a deal for my client at Aston Villa, before the boom in Premier League wages, but still worth in excess of £5 million over five years. It was a decent day's work but there had been a long preamble of negotiations over a period of six months.

What advice do you have for anyone selling?

Don't over-complicate what you are offering – you might offer 10 things but only two might be relevant. Find out what your potential customer needs, how they currently cope without your product and how your product might be better for them. Get to the point – your customer will appreciate you being focused on what they need.

Learn when to accept defeat: What you offer isn't always right for your target customer so there's no point in trying to continue selling it.

If you're not getting an answer when you follow up your presentation, don't be kept waiting unreasonably... give your target customer an ultimatum in a polite and reasonable way "if I haven't heard from you by Friday, perhaps I can leave this with you to come back to me if of interest."

Always be professional on the phone and in written correspondence... saying something you might regret will always be something you regret saying!

Get to know your customers – make a note of something you can reference in a future call...ask how a holiday went, how their son's football match went. Get information every time you speak to the customer so you can build a platform of knowledge which builds trust and a relationship. You don't just call and say "do you want to buy my product?"

Have some pride. If you've been asked to come and present and that person fails to return a call or an e-mail or acknowledge your existence then why did they ask you to come and present in the first place? We should all have respect for each other's time so don't be afraid to point out failings in others...they should have more respect.

On that note, always respect other people's time. If you're going to be late, call in advance. If you make a mistake, don't blame others. Take it on the chin and admit responsibility. Nobody likes someone who doesn't have the guts to front up and admit they've screwed up. Turn a negative into a positive... sometimes it can help to build a relationship.

Confirm an appointment in advance. People forget, they get ill, sometimes something better comes up and they're 'double booked' when you turn up. The only person who loses out? You. So always confirm before you set out.

Under-promise and over-deliver. Always exceed your client's expectations. It sets you apart from the competition.

www.b4-business.com

Anthony Iannarino, Sales leader, Coach, Best-selling Author

After a career as a rock star didn't work out, Anthony graduated law school, a huge accomplishment with three kids.

Like many people, he got into sales since it seemed like a lucrative career. Once in, he realised it wasn't about the commission, it was the value he gave others.

Eventually he started running sales teams, then coaching, now he is a full-time coach, taking care of Fortune 500 companies, speaking at major events and proud author of two best-selling books, The Only Sales Guide You'll Ever Need and The Lost Art of Closing.

How important is sales in your company?

It's the most important part for any business. To quote the legendary Peter Drucker, "the job of a business is to create a customer."

It's important to know who your business is. Who do you serve? Are you talking to the right people and are you seeing enough customers? The better your questions, the better the business conversations you will have.

What skills do people need when selling?

Focus on your personal and professional development, so you can increase your capacity to help people. Successful people invest in themselves.

Whoever shows up to help people make change will get positive results. I like to paraphrase the Buddha quote "you're perfect the way you are, but you can still do a lot of improving."

What the best deal you've ever done?

The best deals are not the ones that have the highest revenue, it's the one that moved the needle. The best ones are where four important components came into play - the client won, we won, we were creating difficult change and the client eventually found the results that were needed.

What advice do you have for anyone selling?

Focus on your personal and professional development, so you can increase your capacity to help people. The most successful people read and invest in their career.

https://thesalesblog.com/

Aaron Walker, Professional Life and Business Coach

For 34 years Aaron was a successful businessman and owner of eight lucrative businesses. Now as a Life and Business coach he uses his experience to help grow others success and significance.

He works with both existing entrepreneurs as well as those aspiring to become successful entrepreneurs and works by the line of thought that a variety of unique opportunities to grow are available for your personal, professional as well as spiritual life

How important is sales?

It's very important and it is to most businesses.

What are the best skills?

Always over-deliver on your promises. We planned to do 20 interviews initially on one of our podcasts. We ended up doing 80 interviews, offering enormous value to listeners.

Listen.

Stop trying to talk all the time. Stop trying to make the sales and start adding value. If you listen, you will provide value. When I went to buy a car recently, I wanted a blue car with brown leather seats. The salesman kept trying to sell me a red one on special offer. He was trying to get the sale without listening so I went elsewhere. Two weeks later, he called me and said he had the blue car, but it was too late. I had bought the car from another garage.

What is the best sale you have ever done?

When the client is pleasantly surprised at the ending. It's not the biggest deal that's important, it's always how special the other person feels.

What advice do you have for anyone selling?

Be honest enough to say no to a customer who isn't the right fit. Once I had to turn away a customer who was offering a huge amount of money, but he was a corporate worker who had no desire to run his own business and I advise entrepreneurs, which is a different skillset.

The money would have been great; however, you always have to do the right thing.

Office culture is more important than people realise. Everyone needs to be after the same goal of serving. Chemistry with customers is so important. John Lee Dumas, who runs Entrepreneur on Fire had me on his show. He's one of the top podcasters in America and I was so grateful to be on his show that I made a special framed picture and sent it overnight delivery as a thank you. He now tells so many people about me and I get more work and recognition from a simple thank you gesture.

Instead of thank you cards after a deal, send a thank you video. You get so much more emotion across and again, customers remember it for a long time.

www.viewfromthetop.com

Jim Newsome, President and CEO South Carolina Ports Authority Charleston, SC

Jim grew up on the Port of Savannah, his father was an executive there. After receiving a MBA in logistics and transportation from the University of Tennessee, he embarked on a 30-year career as a container carrier executive, most recently as the President of the Americas for Hapag-Lloyd AG.

In 2009, he accepted his current position as President and CEO of the South Carolina Ports Authority and embarked on turning around the fortunes of the port, which had languished in the period 2005-2009.

South Carolina Ports Authority is a publicly owned and operated port system located in the fast-growing U.S. Southeast. It is the 9th largest U.S. container port having handled over 2.1 million TEU in 2017 and will be the deepest harbour on the U.S. East Coast by end of 2020.

How important is sales in your company?

Sales is the lifeblood of business because success starts and ends with having a satisfied customer base and growth is an important component of any business.

The CEO has to play a significant role in the sales process supporting the efforts of their sales team and reinforcing commitments to clients. The CEO sets the culture within which the sales force operates, hopefully one of focus with a view to selling for lasting relationships.

What skills do people need when selling?

Selling is a very difficult profession because customers have many choices and rejection is quite common. A successful sales person needs an entrepreneurial mentality where they can focus and prioritise their scarce time while translating the important attributes of their product or service into clear benefits for the customer. Port services are relatively strategic in nature so require a very consultative sell with lots of patience as the sales cycle can be a long one.

What's the best sale you've ever done and how did it happen?

When I joined the port in 2009, we had lost 40% of our container volume and were at risk of losing our largest customer. The port had lost its competitiveness and was a risk for extinction in the container market.

We needed to clarify our message for our clients, which aligned around the fact that we have a very capable port that could efficiently serve the needs of the larger container ships that would be deployed to the East Coast.

Fortunately, we got a "quick win" when one large line decided to deploy an 8,000 TEU ship to the U.S. East Coast early in 2010.

This "proof of concept" gave us the confidence to move forward with our newly defined approach. Achieving "quick wins" in any turnaround effort is vitally important.

What advice do you have for anyone selling?

Selling is a difficult profession, it isn't for everyone, and is deserving of respect from those in the organisation not performing that function.

You need to clearly define the needs of the customer relative to their product and translate the important attributes of their product into recognisable benefits for the client. At the right time, you have to "ask for the business."

This is often identified as the major shortcoming of sales people, not "asking for the business" and making the choice of their product the right one. In the port business, successful sales entails removing any risk of the use of your port.

www.scspa.com

Michelle Lewis, Visibility Expert at Visibility Vixen

Michelle is the founder of Visibility Vixen and is a visibility expert who specialises in helping launching entrepreneurs skyrocket their visibility, monetise their success and bring their unique message into the online space.

Through her courses, podcast and Facebook group *The Visible Entrepreneur* – she comes alongside each student to show them how to set up their systems, perfect their branding, and get on camera for video and live streaming to grow their business.

She's been featured in The Huffington Post, Fast Company, JustLuxe. com, Nav.com and LadyBossBlogger.com!

How important is sales in your company?

Sales is the lifeblood! I couldn't keep growing my business without regular sales.

What skills do people need when selling?

Authenticity, planning, dedication and persistence. I also surround myself with positive and supportive people.

What's the best sale you've ever done and how did it happen?

When I launched my Visibility Mastermind. To see people's relief when they joined the programme and their joy having a place to go to for support was absolutely wonderful! It's my favourite part of my business, even today.

What advice do you have for anyone selling?

If you're in it for the money, you're in the wrong field. Be a telemarketer.

Making true sales, where the exchange of money is honourable and valued, is an immense gift.

Create something that would enhance your life before offering it to anyone else. Alleviate pain, increase relief. That's the key to truly helping people with your products.

https://www.visibiliyvixen.com/home

Lucy V. Hay, Script Editor, Author and Blogger

Lucy V. Hay is a novelist, script editor and blogger who helps writers via her Bang2Write consultancy. She's educational director for the London Screenwriters' Festival and associate producer of the movie Assassin, starring Danny Dyer. Her thriller novel, The Other Twin, was a breakout hit in 2017.

How important is sales to your business?

Sales is EVERYTHING to my business. I've used content marketing online, via blogs and social media, to create an income for my family and build my career from scratch.

What skills do people need when selling?

It helps to be both observant and highly adaptable. You need to take note of your customers' preferences and give them what they want, the way they want it.

My users love Facebook for example, so I pour the majority of my outreach into that platform. They've more or less abandoned Twitter, but they've embraced Instagram, so now I'm on there.

They've got more and more interested in video and YouTube, so I will be launching a YouTube channel next. If I always adapt, I will never be left behind.

What's the best sale you've ever done?

Setting up the blog! It was all accidental back in the day – I wrote about craft online so I had somewhere I could refer my script editing clients to, so I could free up space in their reports to talk about their work.

Then I started getting emails, then comments about my articles online. I'd thought the only people reading my articles were my clients. It was like a big flashing lightbulb went off above my head... maybe I could use the blog to market myself and get MORE clients.

I started reading about blogging and building my platform. The rest as they say is history.

What advice do you have to anyone selling?

Pay attention. Even when something is working, one day you'll wake up and it'll have changed. Make sure you monitor what you're doing and always have a plan B.

www.bang2write.com

Ben Woollard, Founder of Authentic recruitment

Ben is the owner of Authentic Recruitment, a permanent recruitment agency based in the centre of Sheffield that places professionals in predominately tech and sales roles throughout the UK.

Ben started his business on a four-day week to allow a day for chaplaincy work and other projects; this has led to the birth of Emergency Department pastors, which he co-founded, that now has 24 volunteers going into Accident and Emergency, providing pastoral support for the sick.

How important is sales in your company?

Our business is a complete sales 360º. We sell our services to businesses, we then promote those businesses to candidates and in turn advocate our candidates to businesses for specific job roles. There are few industries as sales intensive as Recruitment.

What skills do people need when selling?

Sales is a skill that can be learnt and improved on, like any relational transaction. It's very normal to see the waste when a strong athlete doesn't develop their skills, the same is true when someone with a natural sales flair doesn't develop it.

Time and time again I have worked with, and employed 'natural sales people' who have been overtaken in ability and results by others. What's the common thread?

Discipline – the discipline to engage in continuous training, to try new techniques and maintain a positive relationship in the long term.

One of my favourite proverbs is "Wear out the doorstep of a wise man", it takes humility and proactivity to engage with those who have better skills. I have made it a habit to ask questions and seek guidance from those who I perceive to be a success in their field.

In short, discipline, humility and determination are the key skills and all other sales skills flow from those.

What's the best sale you've ever done and how did it happen?

The best sales should always result in long, mutually beneficial and lucrative relationships. When I started Authentic Recruitment and the temptation was to make quick sales so the business could survive, I was introduced to a very successful businessman with an international business.

He offered to mentor me and I took him up on the offer.

During the first session, I was keenly aware of the opportunity to ask for business, but I remembered some advice I received about relational connections.

The advice was - don't be hasty to 'cash in' on a relational connection, as if done too early that can actually be a 'cashing out'. I was mentored for about a year and one day he invited his HR director into the meeting and said "is there anything Ben can help us with?"

As it turned out we found a fantastic member of staff for them, with niche industry skills. However, the HR director had misunderstood some of our terms (and I'd made the mistake of not going over these clearly on the phone). So, when the invoice was sent I was suddenly (and unexpectedly) at the receiving end of a heated dispute.

Had this occurred a year earlier it would have been the end of the business relationship, however, the trust that had built between me and the owner meant the issue could be resolved.

Five years on we have done tens of thousands of pounds a year with the business. Business that wouldn't have occurred if I had cashed out of the relationship early.

There are plenty of examples I could give where I've managed to solve a client problem and make unexpected sales. These are always enjoyable. The reason I share the above story is that it is an example of following wisdom, despite it being counter intuitive.

What advice do you have for anyone selling?

The reason Jesus inspires me so much in my business life is that his achievements are unparalleled in history. He launched the world's largest social movement, which today has two billion adherents. He did this with limited resources, strong opposition and a message that was counter cultural.

One of his questions, and he is a master of the question, is "What does it profit a man to gain the whole world and to lose his soul?"

There is indeed no profit and no success in losing yourself, your integrity and devaluing your character in the process of chasing a sale.

Modern selling is obsessed with 'quick win' and manipulative techniques. These manipulations and shortcuts often lead to 'buyer's remorse' and transactional short-term relationships.

When it comes to selling, be aware of your 'core', if you invest in yourself and value your integrity people will buy what you're selling and thank you for it – you will be highly successful in the truest sense of the word. This is what it means to be Authentic. But a sale that costs you your integrity, in my view, is a sale at a huge loss.

www.authenticrecruitment.co.uk

Mel Robbins, life coach, author, motivation speaker

Mel is one of the most sought after motivational speakers trusted by global brands to design and deliver businesses-expanding, life-changing, interactive keynotes that challenge thinking and accelerate personal and professional growth.

One of CNN's most popular on-air commentators and opinion writers, Mel has an extensive television experience as an expert on human behaviour and motivation for many top shows including Good Morning America, Dr. Phil, Dr. Oz, Oprah and The Today Show.

Her TEDx talk "How to Stop Screwing Yourself Over" has over 10 million views across 37 countries and The 5 Second Rule, her best-selling book on brain and productivity, is changing lives all over the world.

How important is sales in your company?

Sales are important for any company, but we believe less in the value of the $ and more in the value of each individual whose life we touch. We are doing what we love to do because of them, and we never forget that.

What skills do people need when selling?

Because effective selling is based on relationships, you really have to hone those skills. Get to know your customer on a personal level. Ask yourself what your customer does during the day, what she finds meaningful in life, what his family is like, even if you can only imagine these things. The more you can really understand your customer, the easier it will be to create relationships and develop a loyal customer base.

What's the best sale you've ever made and how did it happen?

Our best experience so far has been the Power of You course. We created this course based on what we were hearing from our audience, but it has grown and blossomed because we continued to be open to feedback. Now the experience is touching lives all over the world in a very magical way. Be open to your customers' needs and be willing to hear the feedback on your product.

What advice do you have for anyone selling?

Really believe in your product and actively use it in your own life wherever possible. Remind yourself every single day how this product helps you to feel energised so that you can convey this message to your customers. If you don't believe, neither will they. Make sure you believe. And I would go even further to say instead of putting the focus on building a product to sell, first build a community that resonates with what you are doing.

http://melrobbins.com/

Daniel Disney, Founder, The Daily Sales

With over 15 years' experience in sales, Daniel has worked from selling door-to-door and on the phones to leading teams of hundreds of sales professionals.

Following a successful sales career, Daniel then launched *The Daily Sales* as a platform to help inspire, motivate and educate sales people and grew it to have over 100,000 followers in just 12 months.

The Daily Sales shares the best sales content across the world, sharing blogs, videos, podcasts, quotes and memes. With over 150,000 followers and content reaching millions it's a popular place to help motivate, inspire and educate sales people and sales leaders.

Daniel is now focused on helping sales people all across the world become modern effective sales professionals.

How important is sales in your company?

In my company now sales are crucial to success and ability to run the business, without it there is no business. My mentality is that your number one focus is your customer and ensuring you provide the most value possible to them.

What skills do people need when selling?

There are various skills needed to sell successfully but it ultimately comes down to strong people skills, emotional intelligence and hunger to succeed. With those you have the best foundations for success in sales as long as you combine them all with hard work!

What's the best sale you've ever done and how did it happen?

The best sale I had was when I landed my first global company and subsequently the biggest sale of my career at the time. It was the first time I used social selling, and it was by accident. I decided to use LinkedIn to connect and start conversations with key people at large companies and it opened doors to meetings that then lead to opportunities.

What advice do you have for anyone selling?

My biggest advice is to become very comfortable with change and adaptation. Whether it's adapting to your different customers or adapting to different technologies, every day in sales is different and you need to be comfortable being out of your comfort zone.

www.thedailysales.net

Recommended reading
Sales books

- Fanatical Prospecting by Jeb Blount.
- The Only Sales Guide You'll Ever Need by Anthony Iannarino.
- The Lost Art of Closing by Anthony Iannarino.
- High Profit Selling by Mark Hunter.
- Proactive Sales Management by Skip Miller.
- Sales Management. Simplified by Mike Weinberg.
- The Definitive Book of Body Language by Allan & Barbara Pease.
- The Psychology of Selling by Brian Tracy.
- Ultimate Sales Machine by Chet Holmes.
- The Challenger Sale by Matthew Dixon and Brent Adamson.

Personal Development books

- The Compound Effect by Darren Hardy.
- The 5 Second Rule by Mel Robbins.
- High Performance Habits by Brendon Burchard.
- Lean In by Sheryl Sandberg.
- Switch by Dan & Chip Heath.
- Result by Phil Olley.
- Living Forward by Michael Hyatt and Daniel Karkavy.
- The Meaning of Michelle by Veronica Chambers.
- The Monk Who Sold His Ferrari by Robin Sharma.
- View From The Top by Aaron Walker.

Biographies of successful people

- Muhammed Ali – Soul of a Butterfly.
- Alex Ferguson – Leadership.
- Bruce Springsteen – Born To Run.
- John Wooden – Essential Wooden.

- The Man Behind The Wheel – Tim Bouquet.
- Ian Wright – My Biography.
- The Virgin Way and Finding My Virginity – Richard Branson.
- Expelled From The Classroom to Billionaire Boardroom – Joseph Valente.
- Lee Iacocca – An Autobiography.
- Phil Knight – Shoe Dog.

Seminars / events worth attending

Success Resources

https://successresources.com/

Phil Olley, The Nexus Experience

http://philolley.com/the-nexus-experience2

Lewis Howes, Unleash Your Greatness

https://summitofgreatness.com/

Brendon Burchard, High Performance Academy and much more

http://brendon.mykajabi.com/

Aaron Walker, Mastermind group

http://www.viewfromthetop.com/isiapplication

Mel Robbins, The Power of You

https://courses.melrobbins.com/p/powerofyou

Simon Coulson, Internet Business School

https://internetbusinessschool.co.uk/

Failing Your Way To Success
– bonus first chapter –

When I was young, life was perfect. A straight A student. Adored by teachers for my strong worth ethic and good behaviour. Head boy at my primary school – not just any head boy – an Indian head boy with NHS glasses, (Growing up in the late 70s/early 80s, nobody looked cool in glasses except Elton John), in a Northern Irish small town primary school .

I was the top goal scorer on the school playground. Inspired by Ian Rush, the star striker at Liverpool, poaching was my speciality. David Cochrane, who I used to hang out with on music courses in Ballycastle, taught me how to bend it like Beckham before anyone had heard of him.

I captained the cub scouts proudly to footballing glory by miskicking the ball – it spun into the net in complete opposite direction to where the goalkeeper was jumping.

My energy and enthusiasm made me a natural leader. Teachers always chose me to lead projects and sports teams.

Even when I took up hockey for the first time with no practise I scored a hat-trick on my debut. My parents were happily married and they loved me. I lived in a wonderful home, safe environment and surrounded by people who cared.

Growing up, we were incredibly lucky; we could play outside until dark and parents didn't mind, we didn't need mobile phones to survive, there were only four TV channels. Mums picked us up from school or we cycled home. We didn't come from privileged families and nobody was rich, yet life was good.

Teachers supported me. The headmaster was always nice to me. The music teacher let me spend time after school playing the piano. That led to the kettle drums. Even when the most talented violist would give a Mozart solo or the orchestra would play the magnificence of Beethoven, it was me they remembered, hammering the kettle drums.

Being the only coloured kid in a white school and standing while the orchestra sat also helped.

But nobody told me luck doesn't last forever. I got accepted into one of the top schools in Northern Ireland called Ballymena Academy, our version of Eton College without the wealth and snobbery.

Being king in a small town meant nothing since I was in the real world now full of incredibly talented kids. The gifted pupils in my year went onto achieve some great things: David Humphreys captained Northern Ireland Rugby team to European cup glory. Stephanie Cunningham, consultant cardiologist in Bristol. Kelly O'Hara, one of the top commercial property lawyers in Dublin. Michael Bolan, author of The Devil's Bible book trilogy. Alastair Herbison, architecture and solution design at British Telecom.

The ball was constantly taken off me in football. The pupils were smarter than me. Everyone had fun at the school discos and parties except me since my parents wouldn't let me attend in case I got into bad habits of the locals.

My father never expressed himself well when I was a child. There were no hugs, no "I love you" and when he spoke, he expected you to listen without questioning anything he said.

"Bad habits of the locals?" I asked.

"Yes. Smoking, drinking, getting girls pregnant," he said.

I was 11! The worst thing that could happen back then is that I would drink too much Coca-Cola.

As I became more isolated, life went downhill. Very, very fast.

We react different to stress. Some utter profanity. Others bully. Many cry. I became quiet. I would often go months without saying a word. Isolation is dangerous and leads to depression and mental health issues from which I suffered later in life.

When you wake up every day wondering if you should walk into a moving bus, it's more than teenage angst. When you can't find someone to share your life with, it makes you feel unworthy. When teachers try to educate you on things in high school that will never do you any good in the real world, it's terrifying.

Sadly, our education system means nothing in the real world. As long as you can write, read and do maths, skills you learn when you're young, everything else is self-taught.

Education barely gets you by in life. Self-education makes you successful and happy. Learning about goals, wealth, health, giving to charity, doing things for others, sales, entrepreneurship, none of these valuable lessons were taught at school.

As a teenager, my confidence faded. Acne took over. My weight increased through comfort eating. I discovered girls, so stopped studying and failed my exams. I wasted my youth writing music and wanting to be a rock star.

Imagine stacking shelves in a supermarket, getting promoted to nightshift and living at home. I was earning £170/week. Not bad for a 16-year-old – and I pissed away every single penny in the recording studio. Every single penny.

How many short, chubby, ethnic kids make it as rock stars?

My relationship with my parents turned sour as they couldn't understand how I could waste a promising future on girls and music. They were convinced the long-haired rock stars I followed were devils that had possessed me, so sent me to a priest. He said I should stop eating meat and listen to my parents. Clearly, he'd been bribed by my mother's delicious Indian food.

In my desperation, I became vegetarian. It made me hungry so I ate more and put on more weight.

Cynicism. Anger. Self-loathing. A pinch of resentment towards my family took over. Okay, that's fairly normal for most teenagers, however, the kids around me weren't like that. They were happy and beautiful and always seemed to have a good life.

My father took me from Ballymena Academy to a local school in a small Northern Irish town called Antrim where we lived to keep an eye on me.

The kids here had rarely left their bubble. They thought the same. They had no knowledge of the world. Yet again, I was the only coloured kid in my year, but this was different. I was the new kid. As a result, the bullies decided I was gay.

In the 1980s, being gay was wrongly associated with AIDS. Therefore, the bullies decided to torment me by telling everyone if they talked to the brown guy, they would catch AIDS and die. Therefore, people were terrified of talking to me.

The only thing I looked forward to was school dinners. Greasy chips, moreish sausage rolls, crispy onion rings and baked beans every day. In a carbohydrate daze and struggling to deal with the bullying and isolation, I walked into another pupil. Luckily, nobody was hurt. However, she started crying.

Since the bullies had convinced so many pupils I was gay and therefore had AIDS, she was worried she would get AIDS and die.

I'm so glad there was no internet growing up. I can't even begin to imagine how bad the bullying would have been.

My father is now a great man, a caring grandfather and winner of an MBE for his dedication to charity work and the NHS. But when I was young, we didn't connect. He did the best he could under the circumstances. His advice on dealing with bullies was to "ignore them and work harder."

When you're a hormonal angry teen, you can't ignore problems. Everything affects you. Living in denial isn't an option. As John Lennon once said "one thing you can't hide, is when you're crippled inside."

My goals were to be happy, popular and have a girlfriend.

As a grown-up, you reflect and realise those are dumb goals. When you're a kid, that's all you know, so it means everything.

My heart was in the right place. I worked every night, every weekend and every single holiday on my dreams because the first time you discover your creative side, it's like a scientific breakthrough and you work on it all the time.

There's an old saying "if you chase something, it eludes you," and I was the living embodiment of that.

Despite the massive success I appeared to have in my early years, my life didn't really begin when I was happy because you don't learn much from success.

You learn bucket-loads from failure. It's how you get to the top of your profession. It's also how you lead a fulfilling life. Many people don't associate success with fulfilment.

They think you can be successful but not happy inside – or very happy but always broke. I'm here to tell you that's not true. Most people I know who are successful and have money are among the kindest people I have ever met. I have also met a lot of broke people who are morally corrupt.

How can you be successful and happy?

Well, it took many decades – and it also depends what you define as success.

If you ask most people what success is, they say "wealth" or "winning the lottery." Research shows that 90% of people who win the lottery are either bankrupt or back to where they started within 5 years.

Money is wonderful, but it's not a key to success.

I can't teach you to become a millionaire, but if you follow the lessons and stories in this book, I guarantee you will improve your life.

Niraj's next novel, Failing Your Way To Success, will be available in 2019.

Index

Conclusion

I've been incredibly lucky to work for a company like G-Smatt Europe. They have a game-changing innovative product, wonderful staff that make the office a pleasure to work in and a supportive and caring boss.

Many people look back on their life and say they wouldn't change a thing. I never understood these people. Looking back there's so many things I would have altered about my life.

The lessons learned in each chapter have been invaluable to my success. Some of them were simple mistakes, others were excruciating. I wish I had learned many of them earlier in life because they would have made me a better human being.

Many of these lessons are ones we expect – grit, tenacity, surrounding yourself with good people.

Others are lessons I never imagined of, that have changed my world for the better – caring for others, showing vulnerability, learning every day, forgiveness.

I was speaking with a group of young sales people at an event. They were talking about The Apprentice and how you need to be ruthless to succeed. I explained to them The Apprentice is about TV ratings, it's not a metaphor for life or business.

Ruthlessness is overrated, being cruel is pointless, having a heart and caring for others is vital and integrity is more important than money.

If someone like me with minimal education, no degrees or qualifications can achieve success, then there's no reason everyone can't do that if they follow and apply the lessons in this book.

People who sell successfully earn 20-30% more than those who work normal jobs which according to the Office of National Statistics is £27,531 in the rest of the UK and £34,473 in London.

That means successful people who sell – in other words, everybody – has the potential to earn a minimum £41,000 per year. A massive difference. I wish you the very best of luck in your journey ahead.

"There are three rules for writing a novel. Unfortunately, no one knows what they are" – **W. Somerset Maugham**

Leaving a review will help others learn about the benefits of this book and your feedback will help improve the quality of my upcoming books. You can leave a review of my book by going onto Amazon, and searching for 'Niraj Kapur Everybody Works in Sales'.

Special thanks:

My amazing wife, Shweta, and incredible daughter, Shreya.

My parents, brother and sister.

Friends, Janice & David, Kelly, Ashu, Paul & Avantika, Kanika & Ajay, Catherine & Reg, Crumpy, Gianluca. James Epstein, Benjamin Pessok, Gemma & Owen, Mike and Clare, Rupa & Garrath, Andy McCalla.

To my writing family, Mark Sanderson, Lucy V Hay, Lisa Hughes, Vanessa Carmona, Niall Cassin. Suzette Coon including the Gamechangers: Rachael, Robin, Trish, Matt and Tracy.

James Scoltock for editing this book while recovering from the trauma of cancer, forever grateful for your courage and strength.

The masters I've spent years learning from: Mel Robbins. Jack Canfield. Robin Sharma. Darren Hardy. Brian Tracy. Les Brown. Aaron Walker. Brendon Burchard. Anthony Iannarino.

Milton Keynes foodies for keeping me well fed while I wrote at the weekends and on holidays. Saf's Kitchen. Sizzlers. Bandit. Good Times Café. Chocolate Mill. Baja Cantina. Spencer Ollington. Steven Dryden-Hall

The brilliant sales people I have worked with over the years: Melissa Wattam. John Scarrott. Dan Collins. Maxwell Harvey. Andy Stone. Ram Kumar. Simon Yandell. Malgorzata Dabrowska. Alena Barford. Magda Covino. Alex Wilkinson. Razi Afghan. Linsey Rajan. Tanny Khan. Leo McDowall-Benton. John Purkis. Steve Shorthouse. Mike Ellicott. Jan Chowdhury. Nick Marsh.

The Marketing Week gang: Sabeena Atchia. Geoff Ball. Gordon Palmer. Simon Yandell. Bill Maclachlan. Marva Hudson. Melissa & Dean. John Kinoshi.

To those who kindly gave up their time for interviews, I'm incredibly grateful. Gemma Burnikell. Mike Rea. Mark Sanderson. Shweta Kapur. James Epstein. Neville Raschid. Mike Mack. Safia Ali. Richard Rosser. Anthony Iannarino. Aaron Walker. Jim Newsome. Michelle Lewis. Lucy

V Hay. Ben Woollard. Mel Robbins. Daniel Disney.

Written by Niraj Kapur:

Twitter: @Nirajwriter

To discover more, go to: www.nirajkapur.com

Printed in Great Britain
by Amazon